"There's no need to cry. You think I'm dead, but I'm not. I'm still around." (Chapter 17)

"I'm great! I love this place. It's everything my grandfather tried to tell me it was." (Chapter 21)

"Kati is out there by the lake. I just saw her. She was waving to me." (Chapter 16)

"This is as it should be. I'm all right. I'm happy. And I want you to be happy, too." (Chapter 10)

"The only way to describe the communication was that she was talking to me inside of my head." (Chapter 31)

"I always knew I'd die young. It was supposed to be this way…" (Chapter 14)

"She communicated that we worry about such ridiculous things here in life." (Chapter 15)

"She said I was going to have to accept the fact that I would never see Walter again. But as it turned out, my mother was wrong…" (Chapter 6)

"She leaned forward and looked at me, smiling this wickedly outrageous grin." (Chapter 32)

MORE REAL STORIES OF SPIRIT COMMUNICATION:

When Loved Ones Return After Crossing Over

Volume 2

SpiritStories.com

Booklocker.com, Inc.
2005

Some names have been changed to protect individuals' privacy.

MORE REAL STORIES OF SPIRIT COMMUNICATION:

When Loved Ones Return After Crossing Over

Volume 2

Angela Hoy

SpiritStories.com

With Gratitude

This book is dedicated to the loved ones of the contributors, those who have "crossed over" and then returned, giving us a glimpse of the world they now live in, and the world we will all live in, with them, someday. You will not only be inspired by the stories herein, but will also be enlightened about these common occurrences that most people are afraid to talk about.

The photographs featured on the cover of this book are the actual pictures of loved ones appearing in our stories. See the following pages for their names and corresponding chapter numbers.

I also dedicate this book to the contributors themselves, many of whom said that writing their stories helped them with their grief. It's often difficult to talk about things that have happened to us that other people dismiss as fantasy. Spirit Communication does occur and most people have experienced something they can't explain. Perhaps if more people shared their loving stories, like those who contributed to this book, we'd all be much more willing to open up about our own experiences.

Cover Photos

1. Frank Pupillo – Chapter 24

2. Kelly Kilpatric – Chapter 2

3. Mary Reynolds – Chapter 9

4. Ken Kretschmer as a boy – Chapter 22 (also see photo 15)

5. Randall Loring's Father – Chapter 19

6. Rose Diamond – Chapter 8

7. Lottie May – Chapter 29

8. Blotch – Introduction

9. Clea – Chapter 11

10. Sassy – Chapter 18

11. Phyllis Edgerly Ring's mother – Chapter 12

12. Grandma Toni – Chapter 7

13. Eric Wallace – Chapter 10

14. Linnie Pope – Chapter 1

15. Ken Kretschmer – Chapter 22

16. Nellie Bickford – Chapter 5

17. Willliam Bickford – Chapter 5

18. Auntie Helen – Chapter 10

Contents

Introduction
Angela Hoy

Thousands of WritersWeekly.com readers know me as a practical author of several non-fiction titles for freelancer writers, an advocate for writers' rights, and the co-owner of a respected and successful publishing services company, Booklocker.com, Inc., which serves more than 700 authors. Friends and family know me as the devoted wife of Richard, the loving (and somewhat overprotective) mom to Zach (18), Ali (14), Frank (12) and Max (3), a loyal friend, and someone who really enjoys a clever practical joke.

What most people don't know about me is that I:

- Was frequently visited by my deceased father in dreams throughout my childhood.

- Saw a vision of the location where Texas authorities would find a kidnapped girl's body...the day before they found her.

- Was told by a voice in my left ear that the space shuttle would crash...several minutes before it actually did on the morning of February 1, 2003.

- Saw our deceased dog, Baysha, standing next to our van on the night our son was taken to the emergency room after choking (and have seen her several times since then).

- Saw my 4-month-old son's guardian angel on our front porch just hours before he was admitted to the hospital with life-threatening pneumonia and asthma. (My ex-brother-in-law saw the angel, too.)

- Have seen spirits in our 100-year-old home in Bangor, Maine on numerous occasions...even in the shower. (Three of our children, even the family "skeptic", have seen them, too.)

- Swallowed my embarrassment and actually found the nerve to attend mediumship classes at the local spiritualist church, where I learned to meditate and see spirits more clearly, and to communicate with them instead of running in fear.

- Have been openly chastised by friends and family members when I've attempted to share these stories.

You can read more about my experiences in detail in the first book of this series, *Real Stories of Spirit Communication: When Loved Ones Return After Crossing Over.* (See SpiritStories.com or ask your local bookstore to order a copy.)

This is the second book in my series on Spirit Communication and I find it comforting that I'm re-reading and editing these stories while I'm going through a spiritual crisis right now myself.

Last Spring, we decided we didn't want to wait any longer for retirement. We purchased an RV, started homeschooling our children, and took our business and family on the road. While we don't RV full-time, we do take lengthy trips two or three times each year.

Two weeks ago, we were parked at a campground near the North and South Carolina border. We'd been gone for a month already, but still had several states to visit on the way back to Maine.

Our cell phone rang that night and it was our 18-year-old son, Zach (who would rather dye his hair pink then travel with Mommy and Daddy cross-country). He was back in Maine, watching the house and caring for the pets. He was quite distraught, telling us he'd been trying to get us on the phone for hours. He'd finally given up and called my sister (whose been to veterinary school) to try to find out what was wrong with our 11-year-old cat, Blotch. The kitty had so much mucus coming out of him that he couldn't breathe and Zach said there appeared to be blood coming from his eyes and nose as well. He'd also lost a lot of weight. I took a deep breath and told Zach that it wasn't his fault (he thought he should have been more alert to the changes in Blotch) and to clean him up, put him in the bedroom, and keep an eye on him till morning. I said I'd call the vet at 7:30 a.m. and make an appointment.

I was so worried about Blotch that I lay in bed that night, crying myself to sleep. Right before I fell asleep, a calm voice said quite clearly, in my left ear, "Go home. Go home. It's time to go home" I nodded my head. I'd heard that voice before and it was to be trusted.

I woke up the next morning and, before I even called the vet, told Richard that we had to drive home right away. He understood and agreed. I made an appointment by phone as soon as the vet's office opened and Zach and Blotch spent several hours there that day, getting tests and waiting for results. We cancelled all our reservations and started driving straight to Bangor, before we even knew Blotch's diagnosis. We had to stop in New Jersey that night at a hotel to get some sleep. Zach finally called from the vet to say that Blotch was just "really stuffed up" and that he'd be fine if we gave him his medicine, an antibiotic.

I knew that the voice that whispered in my ear knew more than the vet and that Blotch's condition was much worse than anybody knew. I knew we still had to get home as fast as we could.

Blotch was one of the kittens delivered by a cat we owned 11 years ago. He was born, along with his brothers and sisters, in a cardboard box in one of our cabinets, much to the delight of our young children. Our daughter, Ali, chose Blotch from the litter when she was only two years old. Blotch's name came from Ali herself, when she was barely old enough to talk. Blotch was named for the white "blotches" on his back (white spots on his fur). Ali is 13 years old now and can't remember life without Blotch. He has always been there for a cuddle and a purr and had been her constant and loyal companion and best friend since the day he was born. And now, not only did Blotch need Ali when he was so terribly ill, but Ali desperately needed to be able to nurse Blotch herself. If Blotch did in fact die after we'd been away from him for an entire month, would Ali forgive herself for being gone while he was suffering and missing her? Would I forgive myself for not getting Ali to Blotch in time? Probably not.

We arrived home late the following night. I'd driven the entire last day, about 12 hours straight, with only gas stops. We rushed inside and I was surprised to find that Blotch's nose was completely covered in a heavy coat of bloody mucus. He was also noticeably thinner, weak and, in my opinion, very near death. I knew right then why that voice told us we had to come home. If we hadn't, Blotch would have died within a day or two. Zach, while very responsible, would never be able to get Blotch to take his medicine (not even the vet has ever been able to get Blotch to take a pill), and with school and work, didn't have time to nurse a pet through a life-threatening illness.

I tried to get Blotch's pill down his throat that night, but wasn't surprised when I failed miserably. The poor baby had obviously been sick for several days, if not a couple of weeks, and was starving, in pain, and dying. After having his mistress (Ali) and his Mommy (me) gone for so long, I arrived on the scene and the first thing I tried to do was force him to take his medicine. He was miserable, Ali was crying, I was crying, and the entire family was sick with worry. Ali tried to sleep that night, but Blotch was so congested that he was making a horrible sound in his attempts to breathe.

The next morning, at 7:30 a.m., I again called the vet, this time to tell them that Blotch was much worse than they thought. He wasn't eating or drinking, and wouldn't take his medicine. He'd lost one-third of his body weight and the twinkle had left his eyes. They immediately admitted him to the kitty hospital for two days to rehydrate him and give him his medicine intravenously. We visited him the next day and I was relieved to see some improvement, but his sinuses were still completely clogged.

The next day, he seemed better still, to us, but the vet insisted there was no change. They sent him home that Friday because I insisted he spend the weekend with us after being away from Ali for a month while we were out of town. I just couldn't stand the thought of him being cooped up in a metal cage all weekend when we could easily care for him at home, on Ali's comfy bed (Blotch's favorite sleeping spot.)

Over the weekend, we had to take Blotch in for daily injections of fluids (Sub-Q's) and I had to give him his medicine at home through syringes. Ali had to force feed him a gooey vitamin substance and try to tempt him with water, which he choked on. It wasn't looking good at all, but I kept trying to be positive for Ali's sake. After I'd lost almost all hope of Blotch getting better, he shocked us all by rebounding that Sunday and starting to eat on his own again!

Despite the fact that he was eating and did have more energy, the antibiotics obviously weren't working. Blotch's congestion didn't get any better and he continued to make a horrible "snarky" sound with every breath. We were referred to another local vet that specialized in rhinoscopy, an exploratory surgery of the sinuses. After the rhinoscopy, Blotch was very weak and stopped eating yet again. One week after his rhinoscopy, we received the devastating diagnosis. Blotch had an aggressive tumor (fibrosarcoma) in his left sinus. Vet #2 (the one who did the rhinoscopy) thought Blotch was a "reasonable candidate" for surgery and radiation. However, the surgery would have been very invasive and, after doing some online research and talking to

Blotch's primary vet (Vet #1), we felt that Vet #2 hadn't given us all the facts.

The facts were that the tumor would likely return, not within years, but within only months (Vet #2 didn't bother to mention that!). So, at that time, Blotch would have to start all over with the pain and illness. The recovery with that type of surgery involves severe pain (Vet #2 left that part out, too!). So, even if Blotch survived the surgery (which was questionable), he'd experience weeks of severe pain. And, we'd then have to transport Blotch to Massachusetts for radiation and he'd either have to have it daily for three weeks (we'd have had to leave him there) or once every three weeks for nine weeks, in the dead of winter.

When I was 18 years old, I had nose surgery (to fix a broken nose) and it involved my sinuses. The pain I had after the surgery was severe and it lasted 24 hours per day for 6 straight weeks. It was so bad that, when the surgeon admitted he'd messed up on my nose and wanted to fix it again, I said no way. I wasn't going through that pain again. I'd just live with that little bump he left on the tip of my nose. And now, perhaps I know why I went through that...maybe so I'd know to say no when our kitty was faced with similar surgery. Cats can't tell you they're in pain, and you can't explain to them why they're in pain. Putting them through that kind of pain simply to extend their life for our benefit is selfish and, in my opinion, amounts to torture. While we had the money for the surgery and radiation, we had the common sense to know that we love Blotch too much to put him through that just to buy a few more weeks with him and, let's face it, to delay our own grief.

After we received the diagnosis, and after we had a family meeting and all agreed that surgery was out of the question, I cried most of that night, finally fell asleep, and started crying all over again when I woke up the next morning. That afternoon, I told Richard I was on "system shutdown." I just couldn't take it anymore. I, myself, had lost 14 pounds since we'd learned of Blotch's illness and things just kept getting worse!

My first reaction, when hearing the diagnosis, was that the pain was just too great. Once we decided that surgery wasn't an option, I wanted Blotch's pain (and ours) done and over with as soon as possible. But, I couldn't make the final decision, so I asked Richard to make it for me. (Ali also didn't want to make the decision.) I knew Richard would be far more reasonable and would look at things from Blotch's point of view...while Ali and I were running on 110% emotion. Richard agreed, got up that morning, and made an appointment to have Blotch put to sleep.

I got up later, after Richard called the vet, and told him I'd changed my mind. I had been watching Blotch sleeping on Ali's stomach the night before and watching him that morning as he watched our toddler, Max, play in his room and I realized that Blotch was still active, still very alert, and actually looked quite happy. In fact, if he didn't have such a stuffy nose, you'd probably not even know he was sick. Maybe my decision the night before had been too hasty and made in a panic. I was concerned that daily injections and needing to feed him vitamin gel was cruel, but Blotch just seemed too healthy to put down just yet.

So, Richard called the vet again and, at my request, made an appointment for that afternoon to have the vet check Blotch and tell us, in her opinion, how healthy he was at that point and what his quality of life was right then.

Richard and Ali took Blotch in (I sent a note for the vet with questions because I cried whenever I talked about the situation) and they returned with good news. Considering the severity of Blotch's illness, the vet said he was in very good shape. He was happy, active, and interacting with us. Continuing his medicine at home was, in her opinion, not cruel, but in fact helped him feel better (hydrated, not hungry, and less stuffy). She gave us signs to look for to indicate when he was starting to go downhill.

That was two weeks ago. As of this writing, Blotch is once again eating on his own and even started drinking water again two days ago! He's still very congested, but he's not in pain and he's purring and seems pretty happy.

Blotch is dying and we have faced that fact. We know we're now performing hospice care on him. He may live for a few days or a few weeks but probably not six months. He'll let us know if he's in pain or if he's not having fun anymore. At that time, we will take him in and let him go.

I somehow thought, on the night after his diagnosis (death sentence), that not knowing when Blotch would die, but knowing he was dying, was something I just couldn't endure. But, I was wrong. After about 24 hours of frantic weeping and grief and worry and doubt if we were doing the right thing, I felt a tremendous sense of peace. I can handle knowing Blotch is dying, but not knowing when. I am very happy to let Blotch tell us when he's ready. I'm so thankful that we didn't make a hasty decision to put him down immediately, without thinking about what guilt that might create later, if we thought maybe Blotch hadn't been ready and we'd done it too quickly. Blotch is just far too alive right now to put down.

Two days before Blotch's diagnosis, my Aunt Barbara, who died last March, came to me in a vision, just as I was falling asleep. She was holding Blotch and petting him and he was rubbing his cheek against her shoulder, very content and obviously very healthy and happy. She spoke without moving her mouth and I heard her voice in my head. She said, "I want a kitty. I want to take care of Blotch."

I'd been crying myself to sleep every night during his illness and Aunt Barbara's visit helped me sleep peacefully that night, the first night in two weeks I was able to fall asleep without the sting of salt on my cheeks, which were raw from so many tears.

When Blotch does leave us, I know he won't really be gone. His physical body may not be pouncing around here anymore and we won't be able to reach out, scoop him up, and give him a scratch behind the ears, but his spirit will be coming back for frequent visits and we just might catch a glimpse of him time and again. What I do know is that Blotch won't need us to scratch behind his ears because my Aunt Barbara is anxious to take over that job for us.

POSTSCRIPT: Yesterday, on the day I was planning to upload this book to the printer, we lost Blotch.

Last Friday, I noticed something inside Blotch's left nostril and, by Sunday, it appeared to have made significant progress toward the opening. I realized it was probably the tumor.

The vet had told us that the tumor might break through and reach his brain, but we never thought it would grow the other way. I hoped the children wouldn't notice it, but Ali did and was distraught that she could actually see what was killing her best friend.

On Saturday, Blotch's condition started to decline dramatically. I called the vet and sent our son, Zach, to pick up more medication for him. We'd planned to take him in on Monday to have the vet evaluate his condition. It was looking very grim by Saturday night and, on Sunday, Blotch started making hack/cough/wheeze sounds when he was eating. He'd made that sound occasionally during the previous week, but it was coming more frequently and more severely. It was painful to watch and we knew that Blotch was fighting for every breath during those horrible episodes.

On Sunday night, around 11:30, Blotch was standing by the pantry, wanting his kitty treats. I put some on the floor for him and, when he bent his head down to eat them, he started to make a repetitious, odd sound and his body was shaking. It sounded like a turkey gobbling, of all things. I pushed his head back, thinking the position of his head, leaning down, was causing him to have a seizure, which the vet warned us might happen.

The sound and shaking stopped and he ate his treats. However, when he finished and turned around, it happened again. I ran upstairs and told Richard I thought Blotch was having seizures. I then called the emergency vet and explained what happened. They said it didn't sound like a seizure, but was probably just Blotch's reaction to pain or discomfort.

Ali and I agreed that Blotch had reached a point where it seemed, to us, that his bad moments were now outweighing his good ones. We knew we'd have to take him to the vet the following morning and let him go. Ali cried off and on and finally fell asleep. I tried to sleep but couldn't because I was crying so hard. I got up several times because I was so miserable and so confused, wondering if we'd made the right decision.

It was raining outside, complementing the mood in our grieving home. Lying in bed, sobbing, I heard a thump. The wind blew over our plastic Santa and I had to go out in the rain and bring him indoors. When I came back in, it was around 2:30 a.m. and I noticed Blotch was sleeping in his favorite winter spot, directly over the heater vent in the downstairs front hallway. Blotch could no longer walk up the stairs by himself and could barely even make it down the stairs because he was so weak and uncomfortable. I'd watched him try to walk down the stairs earlier that evening and he'd stopped after only the first stair to rest. I wanted Blotch near us that night, but I knew he wanted to sleep in his favorite spot. So, I patted him, told him I loved him, and went back to bed.

I did finally fall asleep, only after praying fervently, desperately begging God to send me a sign that what we were planning to do the next morning was the right thing. And, God delivered, with a little help from Blotch.

I dreamed that it was nighttime. It was very dark and I was alone, running down a long sidewalk, carrying Blotch to the vet. Blotch was like a threadbare rag doll and pieces of him were falling off, one after another. I was trying to hold him together while running, desperate to get to the vet before they closed, frantic to have them quickly end Blotch's suffering. But, when I arrived, they were closed. I was all alone on a dark sidewalk, holding what was left of Blotch. When I looked down, I realized he was already dead.

Oddly, his head had fallen off, too, but I still had his heart in my hand and I pushed it back into what was left of his body, wrapped his body in my coat and turned around, relieved that it was finally over but so sad that Blotch had suffered so horribly. Then I woke up.

I saw my Aunt Barbara standing there by the sink with her hands on her hips, smiling, waiting to take Blotch from us.

I sat upright and looked at the clock (something people with chronic insomnia do a lot). It was 4:00 a.m. That's when I noticed a weight on my legs. I looked down and started sobbing. Blotch was lying on my legs, sound asleep, curled up in a ball with his head upside down, his favorite sleeping position. Not only had Blotch been able to climb the stairs all by himself, which he hadn't been able to do since his illness got so severe, but he'd also managed to jump up on our bed! Either Blotch performed this miracle, or God picked him up and put him in our bed, on my legs, his favorite place to sleep in our room. Either scenario was a miracle in itself. I started sobbing when I realized that God had given me the sign I'd so desperately begged him for! My sobs woke up Richard and I told him what had happened.

God and Blotch told me, through my dream, that I needed to help Blotch go to Heaven before it was too late and too painful. He'd been, physically, falling to pieces before our eyes all weekend. It was time and I had to get him there as quickly as possible because he was ready to be released from the pain. He was tired of struggling for every breath, tired of us constantly wiping his already raw nose, tired of not being able to walk where he wanted to walk, and tired of the needles and medicine. He was just...tired. Blotch was ready to go home.

People told me that Blotch would tell us when it was time. They were right, and Blotch's message was loud and clear.

I called the vet at 7:30 a.m. and they told us to bring him in at 9:30. At 9:10, Blotch was standing by the backdoor. Did he know? I let him outside. He walked over to the garden and Ali followed him while I grabbed my coat. Ali picked him up and wrapped him in his favorite fleece blankie, and we took him for his last car ride. Blotch laid in Ali's arms, not fighting the car ride, not struggling to get out of her arms like he used to do in the car...just content to lie there and be scratched and petted. Did he know? We arrived at the vet and they put us in a room. Ali and I started crying again, telling Blotch it was okay...to go to the light when he saw it. I saw my Aunt Barbara standing there by the sink with her hands on her hips, smiling, waiting to take Blotch from us.

I saw a flash of light on the wall, and then another, right behind Ali, who was sitting in a chair, cradling Blotch on her lap. I told Ali about the lights. She knew what they were and she smiled. Blotch was lying so still, so relaxed, so...accepting? The vet gave Blotch a small shot, a sedative. Blotch didn't even flinch when the needle went in. He relaxed more and started snoring soundly, like he's done since he got sick, a soft, rhythmic rumble...a sound that has told us, during Blotch's illness, that we needed to be quiet. It was Blotch's time to rest.

The vet then gave Blotch another shot that calmly and almost instantly stopped his heart. At that moment, I saw an explosion of flashing lights behind Ali and I knew that everybody who loved Blotch who had already passed over had come for him, to show him the way home. The lights disappeared as quickly as they'd come and Blotch went with them, no longer struggling for every breath, no longer fighting to stay with us just because we selfishly didn't want him to go. We had finally let him go....and Blotch peacefully and silently returned home.

Ali and I drove back to our house, picked up Richard and Max (our son, Frank, was visiting his grandparents in Texas and Zach was in school), and spent the entire day running errands, struggling to delay the wall of grief that would inevitably hit us later when we saw Blotch's favorite sleeping spots, his food bowl, the tissues we'd placed throughout the house because his nose needed constant wiping, and the box of syringes, IV bags and medicine. While we were running errands, I found myself worrying about where Blotch was, what he was doing and who he was with and curious if he was afraid of his new home. Did he remember Heaven from before he was born? Was he afraid? Was he looking for us?

When we returned to the house that evening, Ali spent a lot of time in her room, surrounded by memories of Blotch. I walked in and she was crying. She cried off and on all evening, even as we wrapped Christmas presents. Ali and I were alone downstairs after everyone went to bed, when we quickly realized we weren't really alone.

I was sitting in the dining room, updating my gift list on my computer, when I very distinctly heard Blotch make his snoring sound coming from the living room. I was quite startled and then thought it was my imagination. Later, when I was standing in the kitchen, I heard it again. I heard it a little while later after I came out of the downstairs bathroom. I finally admitted that it couldn't be my imagination.

I didn't want to bring Blotch up again because Ali had finally stopped crying, but I just had to know. I tried to sound casual when I asked Ali, "Um, have you heard Blotch this evening?!"

She burst into a smile and said, "Yes!" She'd heard him making that same snoring sound all evening, too, but she'd been afraid it was her imagination, too.

Blotch didn't come to sleep with me that night, but I learned why the next morning. Ali said she went to bed and then felt Blotch's tail on her stomach. And, the following morning, as I was walking past our bedroom, I caught a glimpse of Blotch sitting on Richard's desk. When I jumped back to look inside our bedroom door again, I wasn't surprised that I could no longer see him.

People usually see spirits when their minds are relaxed and not churning with stress. If someone is surprised by what they just saw (seeing someone who's already dead can be quite a shock!), they become instantly alert and are no longer in a relaxed state. If you do catch a glimpse of a loved one in spirit but they "disappear," you should acknowledge them with a loving word because, even though you can't see them, they're probably still right there with you.

We no longer have to worry about what Blotch is doing on the "other side." We know he never really left us. He only left the pain of the physical world behind. And, while we may only rarely hear him, feel him, or even hopefully see him, we know he's right here with us...slightly out of focus for our human eyes, but in no way out of our lives.

Don't Be Afraid...

I was raised knowing there is life after death, but believing that most people end up in hell. So, from an early age, I feared God (which no child should have to do!). At the age of five, my father died. Shortly thereafter, he started coming to me in dreams. I, of course, thought these were just dreams. Nobody ever taught me that spirits may come back to help us, so it never occurred to me to take the dreams seriously or to even mention them to anybody, not even to my mother.

I'd been taught in church that communicating with spirits was "evil" and only "demons" would be encountered if you actively participated in that kind of nonsense.

I bet many of you were raised the same way. Up until two years ago, I was terrified of death and what might or might not be beyond. I mean, what if the Muslims were right? What if I was the wrong religion? What about the people in African tribes who live their entire lives without bibles or "proper" religious training? Did they all go to hell just because they were born far away from all the preachers in the world? What if the Jews were right and we Christians were all going to burn in hell? And who was this Buddha guy?

How could we possibly know if we're the one "right" religion, and why does every religion dictate that members of every other religion are going to hell? The older I got, the more I thought about this and realized, if God loves us more than we even love our own children (a love so strong I can't even fathom its intensity), he would never banish us, no matter what we did wrong, even if our parents or our society raised us under the "wrong" religion.

So, I created this series of books and the website, SpiritStories.com, for people like me, people who are afraid of death or who fear, for whatever reason, they will never see their loved ones again after leaving this world. And, hopefully, by reading these words, you will learn more about how to either communicate with your loved ones who have already crossed over or to simply recognize when your loved ones are trying to communicate with you.

If you knew how common these occurrences were, you'd never again doubt that shadow you glimpsed across the room, that voice that gently whispered in your ear, or that vivid dream that just won't fade away.

Our Stories

1. "She's So Purty"
Anne Culbreath Watkins

Grandma Linnie was the kind of grandmother who welcomed you into her lap no matter how sticky your hands or grimy your bare feet. She knew exactly what kinds of hugs little kids liked, and how to tell scary stories that would take the curl right out of your hair. She allowed you to pick out the most disgusting things in the candy display and bought them for you, right alongside the biggest bottle of soda pop available. And she loved you unconditionally, no matter what. But my Grandma Linnie had some strange ideas.

When I was fifteen, she told me that I was going to be an old maid. Born in 1898, Grandma had a totally different view of the world than I did in 1973. She believed that everybody should get married when they were barely old enough to drive a car, and she feared that I'd never be a bride. I relieved her of that worry by getting married a couple of years later. Then, she came up with a new thing–every week or so she wanted to know if I was pregnant.

A little annoyed, I said that I wasn't ready to have a baby. But that didn't deter her in the least. She kept asking. And after a couple of years, sure enough, my arms began to ache for a little bundle of my own. Finally, I had that baby Grandma had pestered me about, and I named her Laura Lynn, after Grandma Linnie.

A few weeks after Laura was born, I turned in early one night, exhausted from caring for a newborn. The baby's bassinet stood within easy reach of the bed and, as I drifted off, I could hear her softly breathing. I had always been a light sleeper, but seemed especially so with a baby in the house. So a short time later, even though I was bone-tired, I woke right up when I heard a noise.

To my delight, there stood Grandma beside the bassinet, cuddling my daughter in her arms. "She's so purty," she said in her soft, southern accent.

> *I watched as Grandma kissed my daughter's cheek, then smoothed the hair back from her tiny forehead. "She's so purty," she repeated.*

Pleased, I sat up and wrapped my arms around my knees. "Thank you," I replied happily. As Grandma admired her long-awaited great-granddaughter, we chatted about the baby and I watched as Grandma kissed my daughter's cheek, then smoothed the hair back from her tiny forehead. "She's so purty," she repeated.

Waves of love washed over me as I watched Grandma snuggling my baby. Wearing one of her familiar below-the-knee dresses and with her long hair pinned up in a coil around her head, Grandma looked just like she had when I was Laura's age. To my eyes, her unchanging appearance was both reassuring and steady.

All too soon, Grandma had to go and, with one last kiss, she settled Laura back into the bassinet. Telling me she loved me, Grandma left the room. I drifted back to sleep, basking in a glow of love and contentment.

The next morning, my then-husband asked, "Who were you talking to last night?"

"Why?" I wanted to know. "Did I wake you up?"

"Yes," he grumbled. "It sounded like you were having a long conversation with somebody."

"Sorry," I replied. Smiling, I went to tend to the baby.

This happened 26 years ago, and I am still amazed and thrilled when I think about it. You see, my grandmother died a year before my daughter was born! The feeling of deep and unconditional love radiating from her during that last visit stayed snuggled around my soul for days. It was so real that it was almost palpable. I will always be grateful that Grandma Linnie finally got to see the great-granddaughter she had so anxiously awaited.

Anne Culbreath Watkins is a full time freelance writer and photographer. She is the author of The Conure Handbook *(Barron's Educational Series, Inc.), and her work has appeared in numerous print magazines, on selected websites, and in more than 20 anthologies. She and husband, Allen, live in Vinemont, Alabama where they love to spoil their grandchildren, Bailey, Chelsea, and Tyler. You can visit her website at: http://www.geocities.com/anne_c_watkins*

2. In Dreams
Anne Culbreath Watkins

S ometime around New Year's Day, 2001, I became overwhelmed by the feeling that something awful was going to happen to someone I loved. The uneasy feelings centered around my husband, Allen, and finally became so strong that I couldn't concentrate, eat, or even sleep. Then one night I fell into a restless doze and dreamed about my beautiful blonde-haired niece, Kelly Kilpatric, who had been killed in a traffic accident five years earlier.

I often dreamed about Kelly and each happy dream bubbled over with laughter and joy. They were more like visits than dreams, and I always woke up feeling wrapped in wonderful, nearly tangible waves of love. But there was something dramatically different about this dream.

Allen and I were standing in a crowded hospital corridor. White-coated medical personnel hurried back and forth, seemingly unaware of us. I wondered why we were there, and which hospital we were in. Then, I glanced around and saw Kelly standing behind us.

In life, Kelly stood nearly six feet tall, but now she towered over us by several feet. Brilliant white light radiated from her, and her face glowed like the sun. Dressed in an ankle-length, shining white robe, she slowly stretched her arms out over our heads. Then I noticed huge, shimmering wings spreading up and out behind her, and I had the distinct impression that she was sheltering us.

An unexpected feeling of safety and security washed over me, and then I woke up. I lay there, puzzling over the dream, trying to figure out what it meant. I had no idea, but for the first time in weeks, I felt relaxed enough to drop into a comfortable, easy sleep.

As the next couple of weeks passed, I thought about the dream often. And even though I sensed a blanket of protection hovering over us, I still experienced the soul-numbing fear that something horrible was going to happen to Allen. Then, he became desperately ill.

> *I believe that God knew how badly I was going to need the courage to face a life-threatening situation, and sent my beloved niece to convey a message of encouragement and hope to help me get through a difficult time.*

After suffering excruciating pain behind his right knee for several days, he suddenly developed severe, tight pains in his chest and could barely breathe. I knew he had to get to the emergency room as soon as possible.

At the hospital, tests revealed not only huge blood clots behind his knee and in his groin, but also that a clot had broken loose, passed through his heart, and exploded in his right lung. I heard the term 'pulmonary embolism' and my skin turned to ice. I asked the technician if this was a life-threatening condition.

"Yes, honey, it is," she said, patting my shoulder. "I'm sorry. We'll do everything we can."

Gulping back tears, I thanked her. Allen smiled up at me and said, "Don't worry, hon. I'll be okay."

I smiled back and tried to believe him, but it seemed as if my whole world was collapsing. Someone came to move Allen to a room, and I walked beside the wheel chair, gripping his hand as tightly as I could, praying every inch of the way.

Allen spent several scary days confined to a hospital bed, enduring painful blood draws and injections of blood-thinning medications. I stuck beside him every minute, afraid to be too far away. I even spent the nights snuggled up against him in the narrow, uncomfortable bed.

Finally we were able to go home, and I thanked God over and over for sparing Allen's life. I remembered the dream I'd had about

Kelly, and thought about how comforting it had been. Was it a coincidence that I'd dreamed of her standing guard over us in a hospital? I don't believe so. I believe that God knew how badly I was going to need the courage to face a life-threatening situation, and sent my beloved niece to convey a message of encouragement and hope to help me get through a difficult time.

Anne's bio appears in the preceding chapter.

3. Children Are Open to All Possibilities
Susan Romersa

M y grandparents owned property in the Catskill mountains, with two houses and a stream that cascaded all the way down the Shawangunk range and melted into a pool in their back yard - 60 miles outside of New York City.

My mother and father separated before my birth and my mother and I lived with my grandparents. I spent a lot of time in my grandmother's care. She always had a sort of "sixth sense" and our lower house provided us with all that we needed for an atmosphere of mystery and intrigue. Both she and I could feel it, steeped in secrecy and seemingly a living stage permeated by past dramas. The house had been there since the bootleg era. At one point, it had belonged to gangster "Diamond" Jim Brady. Rumor had it that people disappeared from the house during that era and were never heard from again. But, there had been families living there, too, and one family in particular had lived in the house when the influenza epidemic of the early 20's hit the area hard.

As a baby, I had some health problems and cried a lot. My grandmother said she spent a lot of time walking the living room with me. Quite often, she said I would abruptly stop crying and begin to laugh at something or someone over her shoulder. This happened so frequently that she accepted it as a natural occurrence, although one she couldn't explain at all.

As time went by, my grandmother had many different experiences, as did friends who visited. Houseguests reported seeing blue lights rolling down the country road or appearing outside second floor bedroom windows. Things appeared to fall off tables and shelves and drop and break without cause. One woman, staying there with her family, was sitting in the living room in the dark one evening relaxing. She said she saw a child come down the stairs and go into the bathroom, but she did not see the

> *He spoke to Kenny for awhile and told him he loved him and that everything would be alright.*

child return upstairs. After awhile, she went up to check. Nobody was in the bathroom and her children were in bed fast asleep. Who was the other child? Where did this mystery child come from and where did he go? Was this just the imagination of a woman dozing off for a minute?

When I was five or six, I was taking a nap one afternoon and woke up to see six children in my room. They were all hovering together over my toys across the room. I could only see the children, of varying heights, from their waists up and they made no noise at all. They seemed to have great interest in my toys - and also appeared to want to stick together to investigate their find. I wasn't afraid. In fact, I felt a certain familiarity with them. I think I had seen them before, but on this day I mentioned them to my mother. I never saw them again.

My mother found one possible explanation. She was talking to an old man who for many summers had sold berries door-to-door. He told her that, one year, influenza had killed six children of the family who lived there. He arrived one day to find six small wreathes hanging on the front door. Were these the children who still seemed to roam the house?

I mention these things because, from a child's point of view, it is not hard to understand that a life force continues on after earthly death. Children do not have limited viewpoints; they are expansive and open to all possibilities. Later on, they may choose structure over intuition. Intuition is subjective. Unfortunately, we often discount intuition as a source of information because we confuse it with that part of ourselves that filters events through perceptions of safety and/or fear.

When my son-in-law, Rich, died in an accident several years ago, he left behind two young children. My grandson, Kenny, was just four. The week after Rich died, Kenny believes his father visited him in order to say goodbye to his little boy. Kenny says his father came through the window of his room, accompanied by another man who just smiled and said nothing. Kenny remembers that his father knocked over the "pogs" on his bedside table. He spoke to Kenny for awhile and told him he loved him and that everything would be alright. Then, he went down the hall to see his two-year old daughter, Ravyn, and left. Kenny told his mother the story the next morning - and she saw the pogs spread out on his table as he described.

I have been a student of Religious science and Science of Mind for over 25 years and that philosophy simply sees death as a transition to another plane of reality. Personally, I find it comforting to believe that.

Susan Romersa is a publicist and copywriter living in Las Vegas, Nevada. She moved to Nevada as a teenager, having grown up in the Catskill Mountains of upstate New York. This is, in part, a story about a house she lived in and her experiences there.

4. My Grandfather's Visit
Murrday

I feel that the spirits most people communicate with are benign ones. I know with full clarity of heart that my Grandfather's is, and his visit did me a lot of good. At the same time, I know people who have gotten themselves stuck in negativity, both in this life, and after death, in spirit. I do not advise opening contact with anyone stuck in negativity, particularly not when they are in spirit form. Before consciously attempting spirit contact, I would speak aloud that I only seek messages from those who support my good, and the good of all.

I would also have about me whatever holy symbols my own spiritual practice invokes blessing with. These create an energy for good, which is always helpful at a beginning. Let me begin as I intend to continue, in the Light.

I believe it is good to ask a blessing for all communications with, and about, those who have moved on, past having a physical form. I include my sharing of what happened with my grandfather's visit to me, in this. May my writing of this experience be for good, both individually, and for the good of all as well.

My grandfather came to visit me after his death. I was just a child, so I had not asked him to, in words. Yet it was very comforting for me to find he'd returned. I felt very loved and safe.

Let me say a bit about him. He is my mother's father, and his name in this life was Charles. Me, I knew him as Grandpa. I am the first of three children, and I was a welcomed grandchild. Though my Grandpa was, to me, a quiet, somewhat reserved man, I knew he loved me by the everyday gentle things we did together.

I remember going to visit him and Grandma in the summer at their big old-fashioned house. It had magnolia trees beside an enclosed porch and, in the back, near the kitchen, there was a wonderful garden patch with a planting of raspberries. Besides red

12

and black, he'd brought transplants from relatives in Ohio, and grew the most delicious golden raspberries! They had a rich, mellow flavor, quite distinct from the red or black varieties.

I must have been about two, three at the most, because I remember those raspberries towered over me. And so did Grandpa - he was a tall, rangy man and, when I knew him, he was clean shaven with white hair that he wore about finger-length long, which was slightly longer than average in the 50s. Men's clothing then tended to be less colorful, so he wore light colored cotton, buttoned, short-sleeved shirts, and tan, brown or black slacks. He'd put on an old, soft, long-sleeved shirt for raspberry picking, to protect his arms from the bramble thorns.

We would walk between the rows of canes together, me toddling along with a little metal pail just my size, and he with a larger one. He would carefully hold a cane down for me, so I could reach the fruit without getting pricked by stickers. And he would let me pick it myself. I remember the warm, proud feeling I had, showing my mommy some berries I'd picked all by myself! Grandpa was like that - showing me how to do things safely, and then letting me do them so I learned how.

Grandpa had carpenter skills, and he used them to build my sister and I a marvelous playhouse. It was tall enough for adults to stand up in, with real glass windows that opened and shut. The front had its own little porch, with a white criss-crossed railing, and three steps up to it. There was a full sized door, also with a windowpane in it, and it had a clear glass doorknob, too. I remember the smooth yet knobby feel of it in my hand as I turned it, to walk inside. We had wonderful summer days there, playing with our dolls and plush toys. That was another way that Grandpa showed me how he loved me.

When I was eight, we moved to a different house in a more suburban development. Not long after that, Grandpa's health began failing, and he moved in with us there, during his final illness. Dying of cancer is not easy to go through, yet his was a quiet presence in the house. My mother took care of him, and we

> *So I knew from him that the warmth and caring he brought was there for me always, even when I didn't see him.*

kids went about homework and playtime a bit more quietly, out of concern for him, yet having him there was comforting for us.

I grieved when he died, and missed him. Mom taught me to believe that he was in Heaven with Jesus, and I knew that was a good place, yet at the same time, I really missed him.

During this time in my life, other problems went on in my birth family. Without going into detail, I will simply say that it left me having terrible, debilitating nightmares, and that I had cause for having them. I would wake in a panic and cold sweat, and lie there frozen in fear, too scared to make a sound. This went on for more nights than I wish to remember.

Then my family rearranged bedrooms, and I switched to sleeping in the room that had been my grandfather's, the one he had died in. Mom asked me if that would bother me, but I said no, I felt good about Grandpa. I liked it that his room would now be mine.

Mom had told a family story about my grandmother receiving a spirit contact from a loved one, so I knew it was possible. But my grandmother's contact had been brought through by a medium, so I never thought about anything like that happening to me directly. It was just a family story to me, accepted the same as the stories of my grandmother's wartime service as a nurse in World War I, or tales of my mother's college days. Yet, it did offer a place in my family experience for me to believe that spirit contact was possible. This helped, when it happened to me, myself.

One night, in that space between sleep and waking, I roused slowly, to a sense of comfort and peace. This was so different from the horrible nightmares I'd been waking up from, that I lay there for a while, just relaxed and feeling safe. It was so good, that feeling!

Then, I noticed a brightness toward the foot of my bed, although it was dark and no room lights were on. How curious, that the room was velvety dark, yet bright, right there. And then I realized my Grandfather was standing there, in that light, looking down at me. He looked a bit sad, because his shoulders were stooped, yet he smiled at me even so, and I could feel all warm, around and in my heart, how much he loved me. I knew he wanted only good for me, and I felt that he was there to help, although I didn't know how, at first. That didn't matter – it was just so nice to see him again!

We knew each other's feelings, without having to speak in words then, he and I. So I knew from him that the warmth and caring he brought was there for me always, even when I didn't see him. And I knew he wanted the horrible dreams to let go of me so I could rest again, and dream of good. Somehow, he gave me the way for that to happen, because after that night, the terror dreams faded away. I still might have a bad dream once in a while, but not the bone-freezing terror from before. That was swept away by the inner Light he brought.

Now that I am grown, I do craft work. Two Cherokee friends taught me how to make dreamcatchers and I am grateful that they would share their tradition with me, although I am not Native American by birth. I work with respect to their tradition, and I take it kindly that they chose to teach it to me. The traditional belief holds that when a dreamcatcher is placed at the dreamer's bedside, all dreams catch in the woven web. Then the good dreams travel down a strand tied with a feather, and go to the dreamer. Any bad dreams remain in the web, and are melted away by the rising sun. I feel that this is a gentle and comforting tradition. As part of creating each dreamcatcher, I ask a blessing on it, that it may share good and nurturing dreams with the one it is given to.

As I began to write down how my grandfather's visit to me helped me, I had a realization. He gave me this connection with good dreams. And the craft that my friends taught me, making dreamcatchers, gives me a way to share that, and gift it on to other people. His gift and my friends' gift, of teaching me how to make them, join together in one symbol – dreamcatcher. That feels very right, to me.

Let me close this also with a blessing. May you be blessed and safe. May you, all your relations, all your friends, everyone you care about, walk in the Light, both in this life and after, in spirit. May all beings find release from suffering, and live in the Light, each according to the spiritual or religious teaching that nurtures you most. May it be so.

Murrday is a freelance writer and organic gardener who grows miniature roses, garlic, and much more. She has a Live Journal at http://www.livejournal.com/~walk_of_life/ where she talks with friends who are teens, and replies to their concerns. She also writes songs about healing that focus on rebuilding and reaffirming life. She offers these songs in support of others who seek healing, as well. Songs are available at:
http://www.garageband.com/artist/Murrday7

Murrday may be contacted by e-mail at recycler53@wildmail.com.

You can read and download Murrday's songs at:
http://www.garageband.com/artist/Murrday7

5. Connected Souls
Catherine Dorr

I arrived in the world by skidding right into my Grandma Nellie's arms. Mom had a hard time giving birth to me, but Grandma was right there to catch me. Just like that, we connected.

As I grew in height and knowledge, she scrubbed my face, read to me and listened when the world was not right. Sitting at her knee, listening to her clear voice reading passages from the family Bible, I soaked in her fresh, clean scent. Her faith was boundless.

There was always something about Grandma that transcended the physical. She seemed to know when I needed to hear her words of wisdom and when I didn't. In my naivety, I believed she would be there forever, loving and caring for me in her own special way. Of course, that was not to be. In 1972, she passed on as calmly as she had lived.

At the time, I was in the midst of a crisis. Contemplating divorce, I felt a great need to talk with her. How was I going to make a decision without being able to listen to her words that made everything seem okay? I knew her beliefs did not include the breaking of the wedding vows; she might say words I didn't want to hear, but her love was unconditional. I needed to sit and talk with her once again. Her death devastated me. Grandma Nellie had left and I, selfishly, resented her going.

A couple of months later, when my best friend, Annie, suggested we go on a retreat, I agreed. I had to do something to break the cycle of depression and self-doubt that I wallowed in every day. We packed and drove the two or so hours to arrive at the Lily Dale Village Retreat on Friday afternoon for the weekend.

Lilly Dale, small and rural, is nestled along the shores of Lake Cassadaga. Shaded by majestic maples and oaks, marvelous trails along the lake, and a lush park with comfortable benches surrounding an old-fashioned band pavilion, it is a beautiful village. It is a well-known resort populated with spiritualist, mediums, and readers. Magnificent splendor waited for me and I responded; for two days I walked, read, and meditated.

Sunday evening, before everyone headed home, the village hosted a community meeting at the auditorium. The village spiritualists were to be there, readings done, and a general meeting where mediums would respond to auras that might surround people in the audience.

Annie tried to talk me into going but I refused. I had not attended workshops during the weekend; I was content simply to breathe in the calm, meditative environment.

Later in the evening, as I sat on one of the park benches, watching the warm red-orange sunset to the west, my mind wandered to memories of Grandma Nell. I allowed her voice and her faith to come to me. The village grounds grew quiet and I found myself moving along the path to the auditorium.

I came in the middle of the general meeting. There was a hush that one would not expect with so many people crammed into such a small space. Light bulbs hung naked from the ceiling, casting a dim, yellow light throughout the old building.

Rows of folding chairs lined up along the walls and in the center of the building. An aisle down the middle led to the stage that looked as if it was a beached whale caught on a sand dune, one of Grandma Nell's delightful descriptions of lazy people. I smiled to myself.

Around me, anxious, seeking people looked for answers. Hands waved in the air, trying to capture the attention of the mediums on stage; they sat, stood, and paced back and forth, waiting.

Inching forward, through the throng of sweaty bodies, I searched for Annie. Not finding her, I dropped into a seat near the back of the room. Glancing at the stage, I noticed that one of the mediums had stopped pacing. She stood still for a moment, turned, and moved her eyes over the audience.

"You, in the yellow blouse, please stand."

I hesitated, checking to see if anyone else wore yellow, and then stood. "You have someone who is trying to reach you, a person who recently passed." It was a statement, not a question.

> *She says not to worry. She has Will's hand in hers.*

Around me, a chill stirred; someone must have opened a door I thought. I glanced over the crowd. It seemed as if every eye focused on me. I looked back at the stage; she was talking to me. I nodded in agreement.

"There is a warm aura about you; a person named..." she paused, "Nellie?" This was a question. My breath shortened; all I could think was *Oh my God, oh my God.* My eyes must have told her she had the right person.

"She wants to communicate with you. She wants to tell you," she tilted her head, "'not to worry, she has Will's...?'" Once again, she paused; I jerked my head once, yes.

This was impossible. I had signed no papers. How could she know my grandparent's names?

In a quiet voice she continued. "She says not to worry. She has Will's hand in hers. She tells you that there will be much disruption in your life, but you must stand strong."

This can't be happening, I thought. I turned to leave.

"Wait." She commanded. She spoke in a soft, whispery voice. "She is not finished. There's something you must do. She says, 'You will know what when it is time.' She loves you."

Tears filled my eyes. I couldn't believe what had just happened. Annie said later that I stuttered "Yes," and sank into my chair. I remember nothing else about that evening except, somehow, Annie and I got home.

We never spoke of what had happened. Annie tried, but there was no way I could ever explain. Three months later, knowing my grandmother's love was with me, I divorced my husband.

Sometime later, feeling I needed to be in contact with my family, I traveled downstate to visit my mom and dad. We were chitchatting over coffee one morning when she glanced at me and remarked, "I have something for you. I've held onto it for a while, figuring there would be a good time to give it to you. I guess this is as good as any. Your grandmother specifically asked me to give these to you after her death."

My heart leaped as I remembered those words. I hadn't told anyone about my experience; no one would ever believe it.

Mom came back from one of the closets, where she had taken down two worn out shoeboxes tied with string, and handed them to me. She told me, "Your grandmother said you would know what to do with these."

I was steady and calm, but the world moved in slow motion. I watched my fingers open the first box. Grandma Nellie's Bible lay there, most of the gold lettering gone, worn around the edges, but I didn't care. It was hers.

I turned to the other box, untied it, and opened the lid. In an instant, I knew what she wanted me to do. In my lap lay a precious gift, letters between her and Will wrapped with string, his written in pencil, hers in pen. The letters contained the story of their first meeting, their courtship, and their marriage in 1906. She was asking me to tell the story of their marriage through sixty-six years of hardships and everlasting love. What great trust and faith she had placed in me.

I still have those letters and I am writing her story of love and hope. I'm not in a hurry; the task will end when it ends. She guided me once and she'll guide me again; we are connected.

I have often wondered why my grandmother chose to come to me in the way she did. Over the years, my spirituality and serenity have grown. I have realized that at that retreat, with the problems of the world far away, I was able to open my mind and heart to accept her coming to me at a time I desperately needed to hear her. She drew me to that auditorium and allowed the medium to find me in that mass of humanity. The reason it worked was because I was ready for it.

Catherine Dorr's early life defined much of who she is today. She was born on a rural dairy farm in 1941. Her dad's parents, Grandma Nell and Grandpa Will, lived in the second half of their nineteen-room farmhouse. Consequently, her grandmother was close to her both physically and emotionally throughout most of her growing up years. Catherine still maintains a close spiritual contact with Grandma Nellie, quite often allowing herself the time and space to ask for her guidance.

The Lily Dale Village Resort is still there along the shores of Lake Cassadaga, south of Dunkirk, New York. For those who care to find out more about it, the website is at: http://www.lilydale.org

6. I Just Wanted to See You
Barbara Mack

I grew up in a very small farming community in Southeast Missouri. Things are different there; it is nothing to find older members of the community who have never learned to read and write but can read the soil like a book, telling you what you need to fertilize it with just by tasting it or smelling it.

My closest neighbor was a mile away. You had to drive forty miles to the nearest 'big' town to see a movie or go to a restaurant (and the big town contained a whopping 10,000 people).

Our enlarged school district encompassed more than 100 miles and the entire high school had less than 150 students, so I knew everyone very well. Some of them I had known for so long that I couldn't remember a time when I didn't know them.

One of those was Walter. One of my earliest memories is of making mud pies with Walter, putting a worm in the middle, and trying to make him eat it. He retaliated by smearing it in my hair. We couldn't have been older than three at the time.

On our first day of school, Walter insisted that the teacher move him to the desk next to mine so that I wouldn't be scared.

When we were 10, we had a fight on the first day of school, right in the parking lot before we even got to see whom our new teacher was. We both got a spanking at home and three days suspension from school, mostly because he denied that I had thrown the first punch (though there were 10 witnesses, including a teacher) and I denied that he had hit me at all (though I had an obvious black eye).

When we were 13, we were in love. We went to see Star Wars together and vowed that it was the best movie we'd ever seen. We both loved Star Trek reruns and he was partial to Captain Kirk while I was a passionate devotee of Mr. Spock. We passed notes at school, sat together on the hour-long bus ride, and spent hours on the telephone. We were going to get out of boring Missouri, together, and we were only coming back for short visits.

And when we were 14, Walter died.

It was foggy, and the driver of the semi tractor-trailer was speeding. He slammed into the back of the school bus, killing Walter instantly. He was sitting in the back seat, saving a spot for me.

> *My mother told me that dying was part of life and that I was going to have to accept the fact that I would never see Walter again. But as it turned out, my mother was wrong.*

I was devastated. I had thought that we were immortal, and it was a bad way to find out that we weren't. I cried until I was sick from it. I didn't want to say goodbye. On the day of the funeral, on the way to the cemetery, my mother told me that dying was part of life and that I was going to have to accept the fact that I would never see Walter again. But as it turned out, my mother was wrong.

As we walked up the hill to the gravesite, I saw a skinny boy, dressed in jeans and a green t-shirt, sitting on a monument with his hands between his knees. He stood up and waved at me, and I realized that it was Walter. He appeared as real as any person at the cemetery did to me that day. He waved once more and smiled broadly at me. As we walked closer, he then turned, stepped into the thick woods that bordered the cemetery, and was hidden from my sight.

I never told a soul that Walter had been at his own funeral. No one would have believed me, but that wasn't my only reason. We'd kept one another's secrets for years, and I figured that it was just one more to add to the list.

I saw him twice more in the next month, just little glimpses of him, not enough to prove to anyone that I had really seen him, but I knew. Then, about six months after the funeral, I, in the midst of hormonal upheaval and teenage rebellion, had a fight with my parents who promptly ordered me off to my room. I cried myself to sleep while swearing that I would never treat my own children in this horrible manner. I woke in the middle of the night to a hand stroking my hair. I opened my swollen eyes and saw him lying beside me on the bed.

"Walter?" I asked groggily. "How'd you get here? My parents'll be mad if they catch you."

"I'll be quiet," he told me, and kissed me on the forehead. "I just wanted to see you. Go back to sleep."

I told my sister about his visitation, but she was convinced that it was a dream. I knew better, but I didn't argue. What teenager wants to be thought of as different? Nobody else I knew saw spirits.

I didn't see Walter again for years. Then, when my son was born, I saw him standing in the door of my hospital room when I woke up from a nap. I lifted my son to show him off, and Walter smiled at me, the same way he smiles every time I see him...like he's happy to see me. Then he disappeared. Soon after, the nurse asked me if I'd seen a teenage boy wandering the halls. She'd just caught a glimpse of him at this end of the hallway, she said, and he wasn't supposed to be on this floor.

"He's a friend of mine," I told her. "He won't be back today. But I hope to see him again, soon."

I don't know how to contact Walter; he comes to see me when he wants, not when I want to see him. But I think he's watching, and I kind of like knowing that he might pop in for a visit, just on a whim, just like he did when he was alive.

Barbara Mack lives in Florida with two great teenagers and three spoiled cats. Her book, Blood Worship, *is currently for sale at Booklocker.com, and you can visit her website at http://www.trak.to/vampire.*

7. Grandma's Undying Love
Ed Kostro

T hinking back on it now, I truly believe that I had the best childhood a kid could ever hope for.
We lived in a three-flat apartment building in the heart of a big city. My parents, myself, my sister, and my two brothers resided on the top floor. My paternal grandparents lived on the second floor. Shortly after Grandpa John died, Grandma Toni came to live with us, and quickly took up residence in the building's basement apartment.

Between all of these relatives and all of the animals around, I truly had it made. If I didn't like what my mother was serving for dinner, all I had to do was go down one or two flights of stairs to check out what my grandmothers were making or baking.

Both of my grandmothers were excellent cooks and I could usually find something delectable to eat on one of the building's three floors.

Both of my grandmothers fed me and cared for me and both of them taught me many wondrous things, for which I will forever be in their debt. They also both owned wonderful old dogs, and their dogs became my constant childhood companions. My Grandma Toni's dog, Mousie, even became my brave camping partner.

I had found a tattered old canvas tent somewhere and I immediately erected it in our small backyard. I would spend hour upon hour sitting in that tent in the daylight with Mousie by my side. I would pretend that I was a great wilderness explorer and that Mousie was my brave, loyal traveling companion. This daydreaming was fine for a time, but I eventually got the urge to camp in that tent overnight. I just had to try it.

It took me weeks to convince my parents to let me sleep in that tent after dark and boy was I was ready! Sleeping bag, flashlight, pillow, cookies, candy, dog biscuits, and fresh water were all packed up and ready to go. Mousie and I had all of the essentials that a boy and his dog would ever need for their first great camping adventure.

The big night finally arrived and I had to plead with my grandmother to let Mousie spend the night with me in the yard. She really didn't like the idea of me spending the night out in the yard, let alone her little dog. I desperately tried to convince her that I would be safe with brave little Mousie by my side. And, she eventually gave in, as both of my grandmothers usually did whenever I was persistent enough. After a big glass of milk and a few sugar cookies in her basement apartment, Mousie and I headed off to spend a glorious summer night camping under the stars.

I'm afraid, though, that my weary grandmother didn't get much sleep that night, or any of the subsequent nights that Mousie and I spent together in that tent. Each and every time that we camped out that summer, I would catch my grandmother peeking out her back window, or opening her back door to worriedly check on us. She would even silently creep up to the tent periodically and peer in on us. Mousie and I always pretended to be fast asleep when she did that. I guess grandmothers just naturally worry a lot.

I was heartbroken when my grandmother died several years later, since she had truly helped make my childhood as wonderful as it was. And, she had always lovingly looked after me.

Some 15 years after my grandmother's death, I found myself going through a traumatic divorce. I was devastated, heartbroken, and woefully alone. I was also broke, so I asked my parents if I could move into my deceased grandmother's old basement apartment until I got back on my feet financially.

My parents graciously agreed and I soon found myself living in grandma's grand old apartment. It was fine for a time, but I was truly miserable because of my divorce.

I arrived home late one night and, as I entered that basement apartment, I actually smelled my grandmother, and I soon felt her loving presence. Grandmothers have a certain unique grandmother smell; every kid can tell you that. Both of my grandmothers had a unique smell because grandmothers everywhere favor a certain strong soap, or a certain powerful perfume, or a certain secret cooking ingredient

> *She stood there in that living room for several minutes, smiling radiantly at me.*

that they lovingly add to each and every meal that they prepare for their families. I'm also willing to bet that almost every child in the world can identify his or her grandmother in the dark because of some unique powerful essence she possesses.

After I smelled my grandmother in that old basement apartment, that most wondrous of nights, she suddenly appeared in the dark living room. And she looked exactly the same to me as I had lovingly remembered her as a child. She never spoke a word, but she stood there in that living room for several minutes, smiling radiantly at me. Then she and her unique essence quickly vanished into the deep dark night.

Was my deceased grandmother in that basement apartment that night to comfort me in my time of grief, or to simply visit her old home? Was she still worried about me, like she had worried so diligently those wonderful summer nights long past when Mousie and I had camped out in the backyard? I really don't know for sure. But I do know that feeling my grandmother's presence, smelling her familiar essence, and actually seeing her, long after she had passed away, hadn't frightened me one bit. It had actually felt quite comforting to me.

My severe divorce depression lifted immediately after her gracious visit that wonderful night. I also soon met and married the woman I now love. I wish my grandmother would stop by again for a visit. I really do. I guess I miss her more than I ever realized. I also now truly believe in my heart and soul that a grandmother's undying love for her grandchildren - lasts forever.

Ed Kostro is a published freelance writer and book author with a passion for nature, animal, history, humor, Native American, and science fiction pieces. Grandma's Undying Love *is an excerpt from his recently published nonfiction memoir,* Curious Creatures - Wondrous Waifs, My Life with Animals. *Ed has also recently published a Western novel through Booklocker.com. His love of the Western genre was also given to him by his beloved grandmother. Links for ordering either book can be found at Ed's writing website at http://www.authorsden.com/edkostro.*

8. My Grandma Angel
Suzan L. Wiener

F rolicking in the water made me a happy camper, and every day during the summer I looked forward to being in the ocean. My parents, sister, and I rented a small, two-room apartment in an old house in Rockaway, Queens, New York. We really enjoyed it. The people who stayed there were warm and friendly. It was like "old-home" week when we returned for the three months of sun and fun.

Dad had to work six days a week and only came up on Sunday. We missed him a lot, but basically got used to the routine of it being just Mom, my sister, and me. We lived in the Bronx at the time so it wasn't too far away.

One day, I went out a little too far in the water and a huge wave made me lose my balance. To a child of ten, it was a tidal wave that engulfed me. I knew I wouldn't survive. That thought crossed my mind immediately and I was terrified. I was tossed and turned in the water, like clothes being tumbled in a dryer.

Thoughts of my family and various holiday events swirled in my mind, as I gave in to the feeling of doom. After a few moments, though, I didn't fight it, but instead felt at peace with what was happening.

Suddenly, to my stunned amazement, I heard my beloved grandmother, Rose Diamond, who had been deceased for several years, calling to me. She had lived with us for a few years and I loved her dearly. She was always so wonderful to me. I heard her urgently saying, "Susie, go through the wave!" I saw her, too. She looked so young and beautiful, even though she was nearly ninety when she died. I did what she told me and my happiness was complete when I felt the sun against my face again. I wanted to say, "I love you, Grandma, and thank you," but when I looked up to her again, she was gone. How I wished she could have stayed with me longer.

> *Suddenly, to my stunned amazement, I heard my beloved grandmother, who had been deceased for several years, calling to me.*

Weak, but okay, I got to where my mom and sister were on the blanket and told them what happened. Mom gave me a big hug and said that I should stay with her the rest of the afternoon, which was fine with me. My sister gave me a "Oh, you're just making that up look," but I could see that her caring eyes were glad I was fine.

That day, I was no longer afraid of danger because I knew that my very special grandmother, my angel, would always be there to help me in my time of need.

Suzan L. Wiener has had numerous stories, poems, writing articles and fillers published in magazines such as Canadian Writer's Journal, Verses, Poetry Press, NEB Publishing, Modern Romances, True Story, Complete Woman, *and more.*

9. A Big Hug!
Jennifer Hollowell

Monday afternoon, April 21, 2003, was the day before my grandmother, Mary Reynolds, passed away. We were all in the hospital with her as she slipped into a morphine-induced comma. It was time for her to end her battle with diseases and finally find peace and comfort in the arms of the Lord. We watched her struggle from sixteen breaths (normal) per minute down to only one breath every forty-five seconds. It was exhausting for everyone to watch her fight so hard to stay with those she loved so much.

I needed to touch her, to show her some kind of affection without causing her discomfort, so I placed both her hands into mine. As soon as I did, I could hear her speaking to me clearly, in my mind, while I saw flashes of light covering her entire body. The light was white, the brightest white I've ever seen. It hurt my eyes to look at it and made my head feel dizzy. What struck me was that even though I closed my eyes, the bright light remained as long as my hands held hers.

She kept repeating, "You're not listening to me, Jenny. I don't want to go; I'm not ready to go." Her voice held a tone that was all too familiar to me during her moments of disapproval. I immediately released her hands as feelings of disbelief and emotion began overwhelming me. I was reluctant to tell anyone because I didn't think they'd believe me. Even now, as I write these words, I don't believe me. This experience stayed my own that day for my memory to reflect upon and my mind to wonder about.

That night at home, before I could fall asleep, she was talking to me in my mind again about the conversations taking place in the hospital room around her. This went on for about two hours before I finally drifted off. I, of course, believed it to be my own thoughts of wishing I could hear her voice again, to have one last conversation with her. One of the key phrases she said was, "Your mother's right, I am too nosey and I am listening to everything they're talking about."

The following morning, Tuesday, after we received the phone call to come to the hospital because they were confirming her passing, I told my mother what my grandmother had said. My mother crumbled and tearfully said, "You weren't even there when I said that..." Apparently, she had made the comment that my grandmother wouldn't let herself pass because she was too caught up in the conversations going on around her; that she was being too nosey. She passed away four hours after the last family member left and a matter of minutes after the doctor went in to check on her during his morning "rounds."

Though this experience made me feel strange and a little scared at first, as I revisit these memories, I'm filled with comfort and contentment. I don't know why this happened to me, maybe I never will, but I'm glad it did. I was able to have one last conversation with my grandmother in a way different than any other we've ever shared in the past. We were able to have one last moment together without interruption, without distraction, and without all the other things that prevent us from saying the things we want to say the moment we need to say them.

Things like this happen to me frequently. The latest occurance was a dream that happened in late May. I was having a particularly rough morning (a lot of crying), so I decided to take a nap. I was only half asleep because I could still hear the television and sense the cat walking around, sniffing things. Usually I don't dream when I'm only mildly asleep, but that morning I did.

I was still sad and could feel the tears on my face in the dream. A really tall man (my head lined up with his heart) in a perfectly crisp and clean white button down shirt started dancing with me.

"I haven't danced in about ten years, I'm not very good," I explained to this man when he embraced me and took my left hand in his. I looked up, but didn"t see his face. He never said a word. I tripped, but he kept dancing. Soon, it felt like I was just walking backwards. No music was playing during this, by the way. Just the television in the background. His body was really warm, really strong and I felt the comfort I'd been craving for a long time. The tears were dry and the feeling of walking backwards, instead of dancing, continued.

> *We were able to have one last moment together without interruption, without distraction, and without all the other things that prevent us from saying the things we want to say the moment we need to say them.*

Next thing I knew, I was in a bedroom with huge windows and very bright daylight was shining through breezy curtains. I was alone. I turned over on to my back and stared at the ceiling while wondering when the kids would wake up. Suddenly, it felt like someone was on top of me, hugging me with all their strength...so hard that I couldn't expand my lungs. No one was there. I dismissed it, thinking I was still dreaming, despite pondering the kids the moment before.

I turned back over on to my stomach and again, that hard hug came, so hard that it woke me again from my half sleep, but I still felt it after I opened my eyes. I knew I wasn't sleeping anymore. It released me and the pain from trying to expand my lungs to breathe vanished. It felt like I slumped back down on the bed after only being picked up ever so slightly. Then, I felt a shift of weight on the bed like someone was raising themselves up with their arms (like a push up) and getting off the bed.

No one was there.

Jennifer Hollowell has been in the writing and publishing business for a decade, bringing forth hundreds of nonfiction articles covering a wide variety of subjects. In addition, Jennifer has made it her goal to provide authors, both traditional press and self-published, the services and resources necessary to achieve their goals in a realistic manner. For more information, please visit http://www.jmhcreativesolutions.com.

10. Auntie Helen's Story
Eric Wallace

A t age 75 and in good health, Helen, my favorite aunt, died in the most tragic and unnecessary of accidents. She was out on a summer's afternoon pleasure drive when someone carelessly backed a van out into the road in front of her.

When Auntie Helen overcorrected her little car, a 200-year-old oak was waiting, unyielding. My aunt's elderly Ford had no airbags or shoulder harness. (Later, the ironically-named "jaws of life" were of no use.)

Auntie Helen was a quirky, fun-loving woman with a slightly-awry sense of humor and a generous and loving spirit. Childless, she adored her nieces and nephews. She was a perpetual source of amusing stories (often self-deprecating, sometimes a touch risqué), and she'd been a major part of our lives since we were youngsters.

A true Scottish lass even into her 70's, Auntie Helen was a soft-brogued redhead, always proudly speaking with a lilt. She came from the long Celtic tradition of having an active sixth sense, of knowing things that shouldn't always be known, even of glimpsing (she said) the future.

Whenever something untoward happened in our family, the phone would ring well before the news spread, and it would be Auntie Helen on the line. "What's wrong?" she'd ask. "I just felt the sudden need to call."

In her later years, Auntie Helen lived alone in a small town in the Pacific Northwest. All of us went to see her as often as we could and always came away laughing from yet another round of her stories.

Just a few weeks before her accident, I had just been up there for a visit, a visit which later I realized had revealed some amazing suggestions of finality. In a strange way it also turned out to be not a final visit at all.

When our family gathered in Auntie Helen's town to mourn, to console each other, and to struggle to learn the facts of the tragedy, some very odd things jumped out at me. I felt an eerie confusion when I discovered that the fatal tree was just a few hundred yards from where Auntie Helen and I had started a walk on our last evening together. Out of hundreds of possibilities, she had picked that place to park and take our stroll.

I then realized that the accident site was even closer to a spot along the ocean where she'd asked a passerby to take our photograph, the last picture of us together.

Photographs! I still had the roll in the camera! When I returned home, I rushed them to the photo shop. Soon, I was tearing open the package.

Three startling images made my heart race. First, I found Auntie Helen wandering among a set of moss-covered tombstones and crypts. I had forgotten how, just hours before my flight home, she'd suggested we visit a very old and lovely cemetery. We walked slowly along, hunting for the headstone of a well-known artist and talking about the interesting ways in which we note our mortality.

Seeing that photo threw the strangest feeling over me: although this was not the main cemetery in town, it was the very one in which we had buried Auntie Helen. Among the papers in her safe deposit box had been her request that she be buried there.

Then came the photo of the two of us together, standing by the sea, arm in arm, smiling at the camera. Auntie Helen had an affectionate yet impish look. She was a bit rumpled, and she'd forgotten to button the bottom buttons of her sweater.

As I looked fondly but sadly at this image, suddenly I realized that the accident site was almost directly behind the stranger who took our picture. In effect, we were looking right toward it.

And finally, I turned over one of the last pictures I had taken of my beloved Auntie Helen. What had been in my mind in creating this one, unknowingly taken so close to where she would soon die? It showed a short, solitary figure, her back to the camera, walking off through a canopy of trees into the distance, totally

> *"This is as it should be. I'm all right. I'm happy. And I want you to be happy, too."*

alone, long shadows suggesting the approach of twilight. A remarkable exit.

Then I remembered something else about my departure day which had struck me as mildly peculiar at the time, but now really spooked me. At the airport, I had hugged Auntie Helen goodbye just inside the terminal, made my way through security, and boarded the flight. As the little commuter plane pushed back, I saw a small figure waving from a window in what was most definitely a restricted, no-civilians area. Somehow Auntie Helen was standing there. Somehow I could see her despite the confusing mixture of reflections on the pane.

Startled, but pleased, I waved back. My last view of Auntie Helen was of her waving from a place she couldn't have been, a small person, all alone, in a shiny field of glass. A few weeks later: the accident.

As it turned out, Auntie Helen and I had not yet said goodbye for the last time.

Grief is never easy, but dealing with this loss was particularly long and difficult. Over and over, I relived my final days with Auntie Helen, looked at those photos, and more than once, in impotent horror, saw the accident happen in my mind. There were long weeks of great confusion and tremendous sadness.

One night, as I slept with my usual fitfulness, I heard Auntie Helen's voice close by in my room, its soothing Scottish tones immediately familiar and comforting. I saw no apparition (redheaded or otherwise!), but sensed a soft, warm and reassuring light.

"There's no need to be upset," said Auntie Helen. "This is as it should be. I'm all right. I'm happy. And I want you to be happy, too."

Immediately, I felt incredible lightness and an amazing sort of joy.

"Yes, I'm where I want to be," said Auntie Helen. "There's no reason to mourn. Think of me with gladness, not sorrow. Remember me with a laugh in your heart, because everything is all right. Love needn't die."

The light slowly faded, and I awoke to discover I was crying. But, these were no longer the tears of grief and trouble. The formidable ice-jam in my emotions had broken. Smiling, I went back to sleep in wonder and at last in peace.

I remember Auntie Helen with great fondness. Her death was heartbreaking, but her life was filled with love of being and delight in her family. Nowadays I look back on my last times with her, not only with the gladness she asked of me, but with the powerful sense that there were mysteries she understood or at least suspected just before she died, mysteries of which I had but a tiny hint.

Frequently, I find a reason to head to the Pacific Northwest, go to her town and to visit her grave. And Auntie Helen's playfulness is still evident. She doesn't sit still. Every single time I go to the cemetery I have to hunt anew for her gravestone. It never quite seems to be where it was the previous visit.

But always after this little bit of hide and seek, there at last she is. And as I put down flowers or a bit of heather, I hear her voice, not rising somberly from the ground, but light, in the breeze around me: "Everything's all right. Love needn't die."

Eric Wallace is a freelance writer living in Boise, Idaho.

11. Clea
Elizabeth Ann Wheeler

I have always been allergic to cats, but I stopped caring about that the day I opened my front door and saw the battered-looking, pure white kitten my friend was holding in her arms. "I kept seeing this little kitty running around when I was waiting to catch the 92 bus," she told me. "And every day she's looked thinner."

"Huh," I said noncommittally.

"And I'd sure love to keep her myself," she went on hopefully, "but you know how Sid would eat her for breakfast."

Sid was an orange tom appropriately named after Sid Vicious. He had been neutered right after my friend's female cat had abruptly gone into heat during a "play date" that had wound up being just a little more exciting than anyone had bargained for. Neutered, yes, but still aggressive enough to have practically eaten even me for breakfast at least once.

"Yeah," I agreed. "Sid is not healthy for kittens and other living things."

"And she has really beautiful blue eyes," my friend wheedled, holding her up to show me. I only had the chance to notice how much this seemed to annoy the little kitten, catching a flash of tiny transparent claws emerging from pure white feet, like switchblades. Then, I got hit by a wave of cat dander. When I'd stopped sneezing, my friend went on, trying. "Have you ever seen eyes like this?" she asked.

I finally took a real look. I hadn't. It wasn't just that they were bright blue; they were tragic eyes, eyes with real suffering in them.

"How long has she just been running around on the street?" I asked.

"Probably her whole life," my friend said. "She can't have a mother alive because she's too young to be separated from her."

"Is she all right?" I asked, finally really noticing how small she was.

"Well, she might be," said my friend hopefully. "She might be if somebody took her in, and fed her well, and took her to see a vet."

> *"I'm well and happy now."*

The vet agreed with my friend that Clea was too young to have been separated from her mother. "But we'll just hope for the best," he said cheerfully, while the kitten trembled visibly on the examining table, clearly traumatized by the ordeal of having been put in a carrier and taken for a ride in the car.

In the five years she spent with my brother and me, Clea never got over her exaggerated fear of anything that wasn't simply staying safely at home with a full food dish, several cozy places to sleep, and nothing unusual – a thunder storm, for example - happening in the background. Past kittenhood, she refused to be put into the carrier for her annual trip to the vet, so I learned to wrap her in a towel; not only to protect myself from her panicky clawing, but to minimize the mess when terror caused her to lose control of her bowels.

Once, she even created Greek tragedy out of an otherwise quiet evening at home by panicking and attacking me when I snatched her up for a hug in one of my normal bursts of affection. Without noticing, however, I had cornered her. What would have been fine in the middle of the room simply made her lose her head and lash out at me. The slash near my eye from her claw sent me to the emergency room. "Your cat did this?" asked the intake nurse, deadpan. "What is she, a puma?"

I often wondered what had happened to Clea, when she was a scrawny little kitten running around near the 92 bus stop, to leave this kind of lasting effect. She was never aggressive unless she was frightened, but she did seem to startle so easily. And she could be very affectionate, blinking up at you with eyes gooey with love, and then sidling over with her back humped up, bashing into your legs to ask to be petted - but she did attack the contents of her food dish in a way that seemed compulsive.

39

In fact, the combination of her beauty (the pure-white coat, the bright blue eyes) plus her dangling belly prompted my brother to joke that she was like some glamorous old movie star who'd gone to seed. "I know you!" he'd exclaim. "Weren't you in Gold Diggers of 1933? Look, everybody! It's Miss Joan Blondell!"

Liking the attention, she'd sidle over and bash right into his legs.

When Clea got really ill, I don't think I noticed as fast as I might have if she had been a more robust cat who played more and ate less. I also think I might have been a little quicker on the uptake if I wasn't so distracted by a long-distance relationship with a boyfriend in England, who was writing to me every day and calling on a static-filled line at least once a week. When my brother and I realized how lethargic Clea really was, we wrapped her in a towel and took her to the vet, but the towel wasn't really necessary. For the very first time, she didn't panic or try to claw me on the way over in the car. There, the vet wasn't his usual cheerful self, either.

"I'm going to order some tests," he told us, after drawing some blood from an un-protesting cat, a cat who usually had to be held down by at least two people if he did anything this terrible. "But I want you to be prepared for bad news."

When the news came, it was as bad as it could be. We didn't have her put to sleep until it was clear that she was no longer getting pleasure from anything, not even being stroked and talked to, but it was still a terrible decision to have to make and it still left a hole in the household.

I also felt a lot of guilt. I knew that I'd saved an unusually sensitive cat from what must have been a brutal and frightening life on the streets, but why hadn't she ever recovered from it? Maybe she would have if only I'd managed to make her feel more secure and loved. And if I had, she surely would have been a lot healthier. And maybe if I hadn't been so distracted by a romance, I could have got her to the vet in time for him to do something that might have saved her.

Not long after Clea died, my boyfriend called again from England. He told me he'd been for a psychic reading that week and had asked the psychic about our relationship. "She said everything looks fine, that we're very compatible. But there was one symbol she saw that she couldn't interpret."

"Oh, really?" I teased. "What was it - a woman chasing you with a rolling pin?"

"No," he said. "It was a white cat. She said she saw a pure white cat with bright blue eyes rubbing against my legs. And she said the cat was announcing: 'I'm all right now. I'm well and happy now.' "

Elizabeth Wheeler is a lawyer and music lover whose articles usually explain something: the constitutional standard for student searches or the roots of opera in the Italian Renaissance. For this anecdote from her life, however, she has no explanation.

12. I'm Here
Phyllis Edgerly Ring

O n Christmas Eve, a month after my mother died, I was staying at my sister's house while our dad was hospitalized nearby. He had really been done in by Mom's cataclysmically sudden and fatal heart attack and we wondered whether he was going to find the will to live or not. Things had deteriorated quickly for him after her death and he'd reached the point where it looked as though he would lose his mobility, something that can be very hard to gain back in your 80s, and remain bedridden for good. It was a dismal Christmas we all faced the next day.

That night, I had a dream that I was standing in the doorway of his hospital bathroom, watching him as he stood at the sink with his back to me. Someone was standing behind him, the way a nurse would, to steady and support him. When I looked in the mirror, I saw that it was my mother, whose eyes immediately looked up and gazed back at me from the mirror before the dream ended.

The next morning, I visited Dad at the hospital and a nurse told me, somewhat upset, that my father had gotten up and gone to the bathroom during the night without assistance. Fortunately, he hadn't fallen.

When I got to his room, he couldn't wait to tell me about his "coup" of getting up and walking all that way. He told me that he hadn't actually wanted to do it, at first, but that my mother had insisted and so he'd let her "help" him.

His recovery was a rapid one after that, and my sister and I agreed that we had Mom to thank for it. My mirror dream was also the first sense of "contact" I'd had since my mother had died, and I can still see her very knowing look as she gazed back at me from that mirror, as if to say, "Oh, don't worry. I'm here, all right."

It reminded me of a favorite patient, Bertha, a good friend from the days when I worked as a nurse in a nursing home. Visiting her was the very last thing I did on my evening-shift rounds and we'd share big hugs and spend some time together talking.

> *When I looked in the mirror, I saw that it was my mother, whose eyes immediately looked up and gazed back at me from the mirror.*

When I returned to work after a holiday, I was sad to learn that she had died suddenly while I was away. We'd never had that final chance to bid each other goodnight.

That night, in a dream, I was standing in line, as though waiting to go through customs at the airport and, in the distance, behind a glass wall, I suddenly saw Bertha. I knew right away that she'd come to say goodbye. I went to the window and when we each pressed our hand up to the glass, I felt that "contact" with my whole being -- it's even a physical memory, as I recall it now.

Phyllis Edgerly Ring's articles have appeared in Delicious Living, Hope, Mamm, Ms. *and* Yankee. *A parenting columnist for several publications, she coordinated programs for all ages at a Bahá'í conference center and later taught English to kindergartners in China. She serves as instructor for the Long Ridge Writers Group and her children's story, "The Bat is Back," will be published by Brilliant Books in 2004. For more information, visit http://www.phyllisring.com.*

13. Facing Grief, Embracing Hope
Phyllis Edgerly Ring

T he day her oldest son left their New Hampshire home for college 10 years ago, my friend, Laele, knew she faced a bridge to which she would never return. On the spur of the moment, she suggested a picnic at a friend's pool, where they'd often spent time together.

Todd was so busy that it surprised her when he said yes. So, she whisked him out of the house before the phone could ring and change his plans. It isn't often a mother gets time like that with her teenage son.

It was a golden, wonderful afternoon. They talked about life and future plans and, as they enjoyed the sunshine, something was definitely different. Todd was unusually reflective and she enjoyed observing the thoughtful young person he'd become.

Less than 24 hours later, Todd died in her arms from injuries he sustained when he fell from a building on his university's campus. Laele later learned that he had gone up on the roof to look at an enormous full moon, something that had always fascinated him.

In the years since, there've been several incidents that have helped her know that Todd is okay, even if grief has sometimes been like a monster under the bed that she thought might ambush and overwhelm her for good. Each of these "communications" from Todd has helped Laele remember that any love we have for another is never limited only to this world, a world we must all eventually leave.

On the night of his funeral, Laele had a dream that Todd was walking throughout the house and she was beside him as he went from room to room, checking on everyone in the family. It had been a night she hadn't been sure she'd be able to endure, but this dream-visit from Todd helped to ensure she did.

The second message, which resounds like a melody in her heart today, came about a month after Todd's death. She awoke that morning with a terrible migraine. As her husband brought her

> *She knew in that moment that Todd was with her grandmother.*

something to take for it, he encouraged her to try to go back to sleep.

When she did, she dreamt that she heard Todd playing the piano downstairs in their living room, something he had done many times. In the dream, he was playing a very complex, 13-page piece that he had once committed to memory. Laele recalled that it had taken him quite a while to learn it and she had often turned the many pages of its sheet music for him as he had practiced and played.

In the dream, she didn't see Todd, only heard the music he was playing and, as it continued, she grew increasingly happier until she suddenly saw her deceased grandmother's face. It was beaming with the same happiness Laele felt as the music played and she knew in that moment that Todd was with her grandmother, and that all was well for him, however terrible the pain of his death had been for those who loved him. When Laele awoke, her headache was gone.

That was when she realized that facing grief and embracing hope was important not just for her, but for Todd. It was a very necessary part in letting him go on, and in trusting that he truly was in God's care. The melody Laele heard that day has remained in her heart ever since and has replaced a good part of the sadness that was once there.

Phyllis Edgerly Ring's bio appears in the preceding chapter.

14. The Spiritual Search for Mindy
As told to Gina Mazza Hillier by Barb Reitmeyer

Mindy is the youngest of my three daughters. On a balmy morning in September 1991, she awoke with a head cold and pleaded to stay home from school. My husband, David, insisted she go. She shuffled out the door, reluctantly. It was the last time we saw her alive.

Around the time of Mindy's sixteenth birthday, March 1990, Mindy began talking about something that I found disturbing and utterly impossible. "I'm going to die young," she said one day, out of the blue. "Promise you'll bury me in a white dress." She seemed accepting of this, but it didn't sit well with me. I'd tell her she was crazy or change the subject. But as months passed, she'd reference this more and more.

Later that year, Mindy came into my bedroom while I was holding a pair of glasses that belonged to David's deceased aunt. Once in a while, I'd hold the glasses and think of Aunt Alma. "What are you doing?" Mindy asked.

"These are Alma's glasses," I responded, "they make me feel close to her."

Then Mindy said, "Tell me what you think it's like after you die."

I wanted to respect her question, but was stunned. "I don't want to talk about this," is all I could say.

We moved into a new home the following spring. Shortly afterward, an odd phenomenon began to occur. The girls and I sensed a dark presence. It would come into Mindy's room and sit on her bed. She could actually feel the bed go down. Mindy would scream, and I'd fly into the room. I'd sense something, then it would be gone. Mindy actually saw it, and described it as a dark figure dressed in black, face obscured by a hood, more solid than vaporous. I thought, 'it's the angel of death.'

46

That August, Mindy decided she wanted to be an organ donor. "It's really important to me," she urged. My daughter, Cassie, wanted to do this, too, so the three of us went to the DOT that week and got stickers for our driver's licenses.

I didn't share these incidents with David, or anyone else for that matter. I never thought that Mindy would actually die. But I felt someone was going to die and was very worried. I even confided in a co-worker, "I don't know what I'm going to do because there's going to be a funeral soon. I can't face that." I was distraught, thinking about how horrible it would be. In fact, the night of September 15, I lied awake until 4:30 a.m., crying. I knew someone was going to die suddenly. I just didn't know who it would be.

Mindy knew. She awoke that next day with a sense that it was her last, although we wouldn't be able to confirm this until months later. Mindy's cold had her feeling under the weather. I felt lousy, too, from being up all night. At 7:45, Mindy woke me up with a question. "Is it going to rain today?" she wanted to know. Mindy and I liked rainy days and it had been an arid summer. We kept waiting for the weather to change.

"I'm not sure, honey," I answered, rubbing my eyes awake.

"I don't want to go to school today," she said.

David, who was dressing for work, overheard. "No, you're not missing school."

Mindy repeated, "I don't want to go."

But David insisted, "It's just a cold. You're going."

I added, "Well, I don't want you going to crew practice after school. Come straight home and rest."

As Mindy walked out the door, she said, "If I have to go to school, then I'm going to crew."

All day, Mindy told friends that she wasn't going to practice. Then after school, she called home to talk with Cassie (instead of calling me at work, which she normally did). "Mom doesn't want me to go to crew," she told Cassie, "but I don't what Jen to go alone." (Mindy, Jen and another friend generally rode together, a

> *You find a hundred
> ways to create guilt...*

30-minute drive. That day, the third girl backed out at the last minute.)

Cassie said, "Oh, go ahead and go." Jen and Min set off. Ten minutes later, they were dead.

Naturally, Cassie had incredible guilt because she told Mindy to take what turned out to be a fatal car trip. David had guilt because he insisted she not miss school. I had guilt because I didn't overrule David that day. You find a hundred ways to create guilt. We all believed that the accident could have been prevented, if only we had done something differently. As our search for the spiritual meaning of our deep loss unfolded over the years, however, we came to believe – with Mindy's assistance – something quite contrary: it was meant to happen.

For three nights, the funeral home overflowed with family and friends saying final goodbyes to Mindy. Her casket was filled with jewelry, pictures, letters and artwork. Though consumed with grief, we found comfort in realizing how many lives Mindy had touched during her time on earth. Many of her friends continued to visit our home, and we treasured every moment when those kids were here talking about Mindy. It was during these visits that more insights were revealed about her death precognition. We learned that Mindy told two of her friends she was going to die. "Make sure I look okay when I'm laid out," she asked of one. "Do you think anybody will come to my funeral?'" she asked the other.

With hindsight, I can see that I was given messages about her imminent death, as well. One example: Mindy was the last of our girls to get her driver's license. We taught our older daughters to drive a stick shift. I drove a stick shift, too, but wouldn't allow Mindy. She was just so upset with me about that. Was there a logical reason why I wouldn't let her? Then I remembered that whenever a truck passed by while I was pulling out of work onto the main route, I would get this intuition of Mindy in a stick shift lunging into the truck. I also forbid Mindy to drive on the interstate. She'd ask me why and I'd say, "I don't know, you could lose control." Well, when the accident occurred, Mindy was riding in Jen's car, a stick shift. Jen lost control of her vehicle on the interstate and careened into a truck.

> With hindsight, I can see that I was given messages about her imminent death, as well.

Before this tragedy transformed our lives, I hadn't heard of intuitive counseling. Someone had given me George Anderson's book, "We Don't Die," in which he talks about his experiences communicating with the deceased. I wanted to know how he received this information because, from the moment Mindy died, I could feel her energy on me, touching me. I felt her presence so intensely that I knew where she was standing in the room. The night she died, there was noise in our bedroom, a tapping on the walls. The four of us were absolutely hysterical. We huddled in the bed, hugged and cried.

I first turned to my priest for emotional support and spiritual answers. "I thought we went to Heaven when we die," I queried him. "You're with God in Heaven, no longer on earth. So, if Mindy's here, is something wrong?" He couldn't relate to my experience and advised me to read the Bible. Well, I was struggling with this and needed to talk to someone about it.

Six months after the accident, David and I went to see a psychotherapist who was a Methodist minister. I was still seeking spiritual answers and thought this was where I could find them. We still longed to know: Where is Mindy? What's it like there? Why am I feeling her? Is she okay?

He had no insight on this matter. In fact, the only person who derived any benefit from that therapy session was the therapist. We talked with him for an hour, explaining what it feels like to lose a child. He thanked us for sharing our experience and we went home.

Weeks passed and I was still awash in sorrow. I'd occasionally rise above my depression long enough to attend a *Compassionate Friends* support group meeting or read on the topic of after-death phenomena. Mindy's presence was still around me, usually in my darkest moments. She'd make herself known by flicking the lights and tapping lightly on the walls. By then, I'd finished reading Anderson's book. This is fantastic, I thought. I have to meet this man. You see, it wasn't so much that I was open to having the interpretation of a spirit medium so much as I was desperate for answers. I made an appointment to see George.

When that day arrived, I was beside myself with myriad emotions: anticipation, trepidation, mourning. We weren't kept in suspense for long. Within a few minutes, George tuned into the spirit presence of a young woman, coming through to us as a daughter (he knew nothing about us but our first names). He described in accurate detail Mindy's personality (age 17, very accepting, mature, fair-minded, impatient, emotional at times, everybody liked her, has charisma of an "old movie star", that she was the "least of our worries"), the accident (in car, riding with female friend, loss of control, obstructed vision, veered off road, deadly impact, instant death) and who was there to greet her on the other side (David's deceased father who died 21 years before Mindy was born, other relatives who died, a family friend who died young). Mindy spoke to us through George: "I was not shocked by death...It was like walking from one room to the next...I always knew I'd die young...it was supposed to be this way...no one's fault...it was my time...I did everything I wanted to do."
    That experience turned my life around. That was when I discovered that we choose our life purpose, our body, our parents, our lessons...and our time to die.
    I saw several other intuitive counselors after that reading with George, each for a definite reason. The first one got me interested in angels and opened my mind to a lot of things. Another filled in details of the accident that we hadn't pieced together, which really helped us at the time. After becoming comfortable with my own intuition, I'd go to a counselor simply to confirm what I was feeling. Sometimes Mindy would come through and other times she wouldn't. Whenever she did, it would uplift me, even if the

message was not what I expected or wanted to hear. For instance, one intuitive started to sob and, reiterating Mindy, said "Mom, I miss you." That was difficult to hear, but it explained why her presence was around us so frequently

> *"I always knew I'd die young...it was supposed to be this way...no one's fault...it was my time..."*

the first few years after she passed. Even though it was her destiny to leave early, Mindy did miss us.

Then, about three and a half years after Mindy's death, I began to feel less of a connection to her. I sensed she was more distant, and that upset me. Around that time, a friend referred me to intuitive counselor Sallie Christensen, so I called her.

They say when you're ready for the lesson, the teacher appears. Although I mainly went to Sallie to connect with Mindy, the reading took a whole different avenue. (I generally don't mention Mindy at the beginning of a session because I feel that whatever comes through is what is needed.) Sallie delved into my present and past lives, explaining that this lifetime is a culmination of many and is a crucial one for me. She keyed in on something specific that was happening with me—that I can easily manifest things. (If I mentally focus and ask for a physical object to appear, it will.) Sallie explained that this is a result of my having many lifetimes not just here on earth but in the cosmos, and that I've retained a lot of cosmic energy. This resonated with me because, about a week prior to meeting Sallie, I'd had a strong vision of a cosmic being during a meditation. I couldn't make sense of it, but Sallie brought it up and helped me understand why that occurred.

The session turned out to be very informative. Everything that Sallie talked about just fit. The subject of Mindy came up towards the end, and Sallie saw her very far out on the spiritual plane. (Again, confirmation of what I was feeling.) "Her light is very far out and she's learning," Sallie said. "She's studying to become a

> *Some people think intuitive work is the devil talking, or they blame God for their loss. I say to them, "How could it be that God would do something horrible, and the devil's giving you something peaceful?" It doesn't make sense.*

spirit guide." This was confirmed for me during a subsequent consultation with another intuitive.

That session with Sallie was what I needed at the time. Again, I think you're led. By the time I met Sallie, I was being asked to look at myself and the reasons why I was forced to deal with the loss of a child. You always get what you need if you're honest with yourself. It's not always what you may want, but what is revealed usually takes you up a step in where you're going.

In my current role as a facilitator for Compassionate Friends, I recommend intuitive counseling to many people. Churches are valid and perform a wonderful, necessary service, but intuitive counseling goes beyond anything a person can get from a traditional minister. You have to be open to it and have no fear. Some people think intuitive work is the devil talking, or they blame God for their loss. I say to them, "How could it be that God would do something horrible, and the devil's giving you something peaceful?" It doesn't make sense.

Whenever a family is ready to work with an intuitive, I help them find the right person because it's important that they connect with the counselor. Information comes through the filters of the intuitive, so what kind of person is he or she? What are their morals and motives for doing the work? Is it for your benefit or for theirs? Once you start working on yourself, you'll know which counselor is right for you. And as you grow and go along, you'll have different questions.

Speaking for ourselves, intuitive counseling has been instrumental in helping my family come to a place of understanding about Mindy's death. You eventually find that place if you keep searching. You do. Nothing can physically bring back your child, but you find what you need to settle you. For us, that meant learning the lesson behind the loss. In Mindy's case, I believe her leaving early was for David's and my growth. It has changed us in so many positive ways. Our priorities have completely changed, which has altered our lifestyle for the better. For example, working as an interior designer became impossible for me. I still see beauty in material things, but when a customer would get hysterical over a pillow or sofa that can be replaced, I wanted to scream, "It's not important!" Eventually, I quit my job to help others who've lost children. It took six years to accept that Mindy's death was for our growth, and I'm glad that no one said that to me before I was ready to hear it. Now I can acknowledge the truth in it.

Edgar Cayce was once asked, "Is there such a thing as destiny? Is our life predetermined or can we change it?" He responded, "Yes to all of them." There isn't an absolute law that dictates your destiny. It's much more complex. I believe that there is an opportunity for us to leave at a specific time. If you decide to bypass that opportunity, another chance arises at a later time. In Mindy's case, her soul chose how she was going to die before she came to earth. She had remembrances of this choice and was prepared to carry it out. She went with what she had planned.

In fact, the days following her death played out as if Mindy was orchestrating from above. The morning after the accident, I looked out the back door window and noticed the weather had finally changed. It was raining. David and I talked to the priest and funeral director about arrangements, while my daughter Shannon, her best friend, and my sister went to buy Mindy's burial dress. They decided on a tea length, white lace dress and took it directly to the funeral director. The morning of the burial service, I reminded David that I'd told Mindy she could have my wedding rings some day, so I put the rings on her finger. Meanwhile, the church was filling up. My mother, a soloist, didn't think she could sing but at the last minute decided on Ave Maria. Shannon had chosen Mindy's favorite verse: "Love is patient, love is kind..." from I Corinthians, a common wedding verse. During the service, the priest gave a sermon in which he talked about Mindy being a bride of God and that this was her wedding day. Afterwards, he said to us, "Do you realize that I didn't know about any of this—the white dress, your wedding rings, the Ave Maria, Shannon's choice of verse—when I wrote that sermon?"

When we went in for the service, it was nearly 90 degrees outside, very odd for September 20th. By the time we arrived at the cemetery, it was noticeably colder. I looked up and saw a dark cloud hovering over us, but it appeared sunny everywhere else. As the priest blessed the casket with holy water, raindrops began to fall, then stopped as soon as the prayer ended. Three people, all standing on the hillside at different places, saw three snowflakes fall from the cloud. Big, white snowflakes. (They each told me this at separate times later.) Then, as soon as the ceremony was done, the cloud disappeared and it became so warm I had to take off my suit jacket.

Someday, only after David and I are reunited with Mindy, all of our questions will be answered. When we die, all of the things we're so concerned with now aren't going to matter. Yet there are certain things we want and need to know now. If something's important enough, you'll find your answers.

Just remember that you have the choice to decide what you need, and no counselor should tell you what to do with absolution. For example, Sallie got me interested in wanting to further research my past lives. Another intuitive, Greg Kehn, asked me, "Why do you need to know about past lives?" I answered, "Because the knowledge is there for me to gain for my own growth." It was important to me, so I overrode Greg. By the same token, I've learned to not question the messenger and simply look at the message. During another appointment with Greg, he remarked, "You're starting to question a lot of the spiritual reading you've been doing." At that time, I was. Some of what I'd read didn't make sense. "Stop reading for a while," he advised. "You know exactly what you need to know for now. You're only confusing yourself."

I stubbornly told David after that session, "I'm not going to stop reading because I want my answers." But Greg was right, I was confusing myself. So, approach intuitive counseling with an open heart and mind, but remember that you have free will.

Mindy had (and still does have) free will, too, and she exercised it through the choices she made leading up to her death. Four hours after she passed, the coroner released her body and doctors used her heart valves for two people, her long bones for bone grafts, and some skin from her legs and arms for skin grafts. She chose to become a donor and, as a result, the lives of others were saved, enhanced, healed.

In subtle ways, Mindy tried to prepare us for her untimely death. She didn't blurt out, "Mom, I'm going to die today," but she did say her goodbyes the night before. It happened that David was home early from work that night, so we all had dinner together. We cleaned up the kitchen and then sat around, talking. Mindy would always sit right up against me or put her head on my shoulder. Sometimes, she'd tease me about my hair. That night, she looked into my eyes and said, "Mom, you don't really look like a Q-tip. You're beautiful and I love you so much!" Then she hugged me hard. She did this with David, too. She took a flying leap into his arms. That was our last conversation, because I got tied up on a phone call. Mindy came in several times and said, "Mom, I need to talk to you, please come to my room." When I finally hung up, she was already asleep.

When something happens that shakes your world apart, you may blame God, blame others, blame the circumstances, and become bitter throughout your efforts to make sense of it. Why did this happen? What could I ever have done to deserve this? All these questions go through your mind. Then once you've figured out why your child left, you start searching and questioning why you're still here. You look at how it affects everyone. Hundreds of people are involved, not just yourself. You eventually start wondering: What's my mission? What did I come to do? If I'm still here, then

> *You can choose to work hard to make sense of a loss, or you can turn inward and die. I've met people who just exist, and I don't want to be there. I want to survive.*

what haven't I accomplished yet? It goes all the way around and comes back to you. You can choose to work hard to make sense of a loss, or you can turn inward and die. I've met people who just exist, and I don't want to be there. I want to survive. I want to continually grow and help others, just as Mindy continues to grow and help others on the other side. In doing so, I honor and cherish this precious gift of insight given to me by Mindy, my baby girl.

More stories like this are included in Gina Mazza Hillier's book, The Highest and The Best (ISBN 0-7388-4190-0). The book introduces a powerful means of living through inner wisdom, and presents intuition as medicine that can be used to bring optimal wellness to the body, mind and spirit. Gina is a writer and editor with a special focus on meaningful living, metaphysics and consciousness studies. She has bylined hundreds of articles in daily newspapers, national magazines and online publications. Visit http://www.ginawriter.com or email inspire@zoominternet.net.

Editor's Note: You can more about *Compassionate Friends* at: http://www.compassionatefriends.org/

15. We Worry About Such Ridiculous Things
Simon Kheifets

M y grandmother, with whom I was very close, decided she wanted to live by the sea. So in March 2002, she moved from Canberra to Bateman's Bay. My grandmother was often overly obsessive when it came to cleanliness, and her laundry and sheets, towels and washing were always like nothing I could ever achieve, and also had this pleasant, comforting smell to them. When she moved, she couldn't take everything with her, so she distributed any non-essentials amongst our family.

Soon after she left, one day I found myself changing my bed sheets and replacing them with a set of my grandma's, which she had left me. The pleasant smell, softness, and freshness of the linen immediately struck me and I felt the need to call my grandma just to tell her how much she meant to me. Unfortunately, I never got around to doing it.

My wife was in interstate on business and I remember sitting up late at night, waiting for her to call. But, I was just so tired, despite being a little anxious at being in the house by myself, I managed to drift off to sleep only to awake sometime later, with the feeling that I absolutely was not alone. I can't describe what I felt and saw. All I can say is that a "glassy" image appeared to hover above my bed, almost like a large, transparent orb. I could feel its presence more than anything and looked at the bedside clock so I could recall in the morning my strong feelings of what was going on and the time at which it had occurred; 12.47 a.m. on a Tuesday morning. The glassy orb seemed to move above my necklace, which my grandmother bought me. Its presence was uncanny.

The next day, embarrassed, I recalled to a friend my experience and we laughed it off as some crazy dream. However, inside, the experience frightened me, so I decided to go spend a few nights at my parents' house. I hadn't told them what I saw and felt until I was having a discussion with my father around 9:45 a.m. on

> *She communicated that we worry about such ridiculous things here in life, and waste our time on anguish and bitterness, instead of love.*

Thursday morning. Within 15 minutes, we received a phone call saying that Granny had passed away and had been found in her new home on the Coast.

After getting over the shock of her death, all the normal procedures took place. Autopsies were arranged and time of death was estimated at roughly the Monday evening/Tuesday morning time, around which my experiences took place. I begged my mother not to tell anyone about this experience. However, she did share it with my inquisitive sister. My sister called me later on to say that she, too, had experienced a strange presence whilst sleeping at almost the exact same time as I did. I only wish I had contacted my grandma when I was changing my bed sheets to talk to her for one last time. She was a loving grandmother and I miss her dearly.

Several months down the track, I had an amazing dream in the early hours of the morning. I saw my grandma. Her hair had grown as much as it would have in the time since she had passed away, and she had an air of calm collectedness on her face. She seemed to be totally at peace with the world. The bone and heart problems that had plagued her for many years, and the pain of which was evident in her eyes, was totally gone. She had a certain inner harmony that I hope to one day attain. I told her that I couldn't believe she was here and she thought it quite amusing. Then I felt she communicated that we worry about such ridiculous things here in life, and waste our time on anguish and bitterness, instead of love. The meaning and force behind what she was saying was far too strong and pure for me to comprehend. This dream had occurred after a particularly miserable day, one of those days when just nothing seemed to go right. But she had a calming effect on me, and reassured me that everything will be all right.

Prior to these experiences, I had always been rather skeptical about people recounting their stories of supernatural experiences, whereas now, I actually stop and listen, as I can relate to their experiences. That dream altered my outlook on life, as it has done similarly for my sister. I hope Granny visits soon again...

Simon Kheifets was born in 1979 in Moscow, Russia. At the age of eight, his family moved to Australia, where he currently resides. In 2000, he married his high school sweetheart, and he is currently studying law at university. He speaks four languages: English, Russian, French, and Japanese. Simon plans on having children, and is also interested in one day visiting his family left behind in Russia.

16. A Shimmering Vision at the Lake
Renie Burghardt

I was a child of World War II, having been born in Hungary. My young mother died a couple of weeks after my birth, and my father was away because of the war. So, I was being raised by my maternal grandparents.

When you're a child of war, you're never sure what the next minute, next hour, or next day may bring. All you can do is hope and pray that it will all soon be over. That's what I did, day after day.

We lived in the Bacska region of Hungary, near the Serbian border. In the spring of 1944, Tito's communist Partisans were closing in and many Hungarians decided to leave. We were no exception.

Grandfather conferred with his youngest brother, Tamas, and our two families made plans to go to Kalocsa, where great Uncle Peter, my grandfather's oldest brother, lived. I was eight at the time and was happy that we'd be going together, since Uncle Tamas' youngest daughter, Kati, was my age, and was the closest thing to a sister I would ever have. We had been inseparable all our lives.

The following couple of days were taken up with packing the few things we would be taking along. Most of our belongings were to be left behind. Grandmother agreed that I could take two of my favorite storybooks with me; the rest of my toys and books would have to be left behind.

"We can read to each other on the train," I told Kati. Reading was my favorite pastime.

"Yes, and we can watch the scenery. The train will go right by Lake Balaton!" Kati said excitedly.

Lake Balaton was Hungary's largest lake. We had learned about it in school, but had never seen it, so this was something we looked forward to. Kati and I also looked forward to seeing our cousin, Agi, Uncle Peter's youngest child, whom we hardly knew.

She was nine and, in a letter to us, she wrote that she couldn't wait to see us.

That night, before we were to leave for the train station, Grandfather suddenly had an abrupt change of plans, because of a feeling he had. "We are not taking the train. We are going in the wagon, instead," he announced.

"But it will take you seven days by wagon. By train, you'll be there in three days," said Uncle Tamas.

"I know, I know. But we can pack much more into the wagon and take it along. We have very little money left. Things are expensive. Why leave the few things we still have behind? Besides, I have a bad feeling about the train. You shouldn't take the train either."

"Well, we are taking the train just as we planned, so we will be seeing you in about seven days," was the last thing Uncle Tamas said before he left for home and Kati and we said our sad goodbyes.

Of course, I was upset by Grandfather's change of plans. It meant that Kati and I would not be traveling together. And it also meant that Kati would get to Agi's house long before I did. That made me feel a bit envious of her. But I knew that once Grandfather made up his mind about something, there would be no changing it, whether I liked it or not.

All night that night my grandparents worked on packing things into that horse-drawn wagon. (Cars were still a rarity in our part of the world back then.) Then, early the following morning, while the guns of the Partisans could be heard in the distant hills, we boarded the wagon and left the village of our birth, for good.

Once the wagon was on the road and I was comfortably snuggled into my featherbed in the back of the wagon, the journey got more interesting. There were hundreds of people on the road with their wagons, all of them hoping to find some safety somewhere in our country. When we heard war planes approaching, we'd all scramble out of our wagons and run and lie

61

> *"Kati is out there by the lake," I said, "I just saw her. She was waving to me."*

down in a ditch, just in case those silver cigars above us would decide to drop some bombs on us.

At night, we camped together, somewhere along the road, and the men built little fires so the women could cook their meager suppers. And again, if news was heard that warplanes were heading our way, people rushed to put out the fires and ran for ditches or the nearby woods, with prayers on their breath!

On the fifth day of our journey, we reached Lake Balaton. I gazed at the shimmering waters and thought of Kati and how she and Agi must already be having fun together in Kalocsa. There were beautiful villas along the lake, too, and I wondered if the people living in them felt safer in their placid lake homes. Grandfather said he doubted it.

We found a public area of the lake and took the horses for a drink while we washed our hands and faces for the first time in days. Then we settled down to spend the night there, before joining the posse of wagons again the following morning.

As I lay on my featherbed in the wagon, I could see the moonlight casting silver beams on the waters of the lake. It was such a beautiful, tranquil setting that I forgot all about the dangers and hardships of war. Suddenly, I heard a voice calling my name and I sat up and saw her. It was Kati, smiling and waving at me on the edge of the lake, her entire being shimmering, as if she was an angel. She looked so happy and beautiful.

"Kati," I called to her. "I'm so happy, Kati, you're here, too. I thought you were in Kalocsa already." At that point, my grandmother, who was asleep next to me, woke up and sat up too.

"I don't see anything," Grandma said. "You must have been dreaming. But you will see Kati in two days, sweetheart. Go back to sleep now."

I looked to the area where I had seen Kati standing but she was no longer there, so I decided that Grandma was right, it must have been a dream. I fell asleep, remembering Kati's smiling, shimmering face, happy that we'd be together again soon. And the following morning, we were on our way again, before the sun came up.

Finally, after what seemed like an eternity to an eight-year-old, we arrived in the city of Kalocsa, and soon pulled into Uncle Peter's property. Uncle Peter and Aunt Roszi came running out of the house to greet us, followed by my cousin Agi, and her teenage brother, Imre.

"Where are Tamas and his family?" I heard Grandfather ask, as I was getting ready to jump to the ground.

"You mean you haven't heard?" Uncle Peter asked, his expression turning grave.

"Heard what?"

The train they were traveling on got hit by bombs. Everyone on that train was killed, blown to beyond recognition. It was on the radio. I thought you knew by now."

I'll never forget my grandfather's reaction upon hearing the news that his "baby" brother was gone. He buried his face in his hands and sobbed uncontrollably. It was the first time I had seen him cry.

"I told him I had a bad feeling about taking the train, but he wouldn't listen," Grandfather kept saying over and over, while Grandmother held me close and tried her best to comfort me, for I was crying, too. But there was no comfort in anything anyone did or said, as far as I was concerned. Kati was gone. But why, why did it have to happen to Kati, I kept asking my grandmother.

Grandma took me in her arms that evening, and tried to console me. "Remember the dream you had of Kati at the lake?" she asked gently.

"Oh, yes, I remember," I sobbed.

"Well, I think I was wrong. I don't think it was a dream, after all. Kati came to say goodbye to you. She wanted you to know that

63

she was all right and happy. Remember, she is an angel now, and is with God in Heaven. She wanted to say goodbye though, because she loves you."

And Grandma's words did console me, at last, for I knew she was right. Kati was in Heaven now, with God, but she had come to say goodbye to me. And as I remembered her in all her shimmering beauty at the lake, I knew that one day she and I would be together again.

Renie Burghardt, who was born in Hungary, is a freelance writer. She has contributed stories to many books and magazines such as Chicken Soup for the Christian Family Soul, Chicken Soup for the Horse Lover's Soul, *three* Cup of Comfort *Books, several* Chocolate for Women *books, over a dozen* Guideposts *books,* God's Way for Women, *two* God Allows U-Turns *titles,* Real Stories of Spirit Communication – Volume 1, *and others. Her stories have been published in magazines such as:* Angels on Earth, Mature Living, Fate, Whispers from Heaven, Missouri Life, *and more. She lives in the country and loves nature, animals, gardening, reading, music, writing, and spending time with her family and friends.*

17. A Soldier Comes Home
Shirley Wetzel

M y cousin, Billy, was born in May of 1946; I arrived four months later. I'm not sure when we first started bugging each other, but it was probably long before we were out of diapers. Because our fathers were in the military in our earlier years, our paths didn't really cross that much until grade school, when Uncle Bill retired to the farm near Dublin, Texas and my dad became a landlubber in Dallas. By then, Uncle Bill and Aunt Loez had added two daughters, Sharon and Beth, to the family and I had someone to play with on our frequent trips to Grandma Stewart's house and Uncle Bill's farm.

Billy's main aim in life seemed to be to torment the three of us and he did a fine job of it. He shooed poisonous snakes our way, dunked us in the creek, and tried to tip us over when we were inside the outhouse. Billy was big and strong and full of the devil in those days. Did we retaliate? Three sweet, peace-loving little girls? You bet we did! Did I love my troublesome cousin? I'd never have told him so, but I did. I knew he felt the same way about me.

Childhood finally ended, and Billy's devilish behavior became mild teasing. During our high school years, we actually became friends. After high school, I went off to college and Billy went off to war. After surviving two tours in Vietnam, he decided to make a career of the Army. Years passed when we didn't see each other but his parents always kept me posted. During one visit, my uncle told me about Billy's plans to retire after twenty years in the Army. "I don't think he'll make it to twenty, though." I thought that statement was odd, and asked him why he felt like that. He said he didn't really know except that Billy had been heavily exposed to Agent Orange in Vietnam and he was developing related health problems.

One month before his retirement from the service, Billy returned to Texas to visit with his folks for a few days. On a sultry June morning, the ancient air conditioning unit in his parents' living room went on the blink. Billy was heading for Houston to pick up his teenage daughter, taking his three-year-old, Karen Loez, with him. He told his mother, "Don't worry, Mama, I'll fix the air conditioner when I get back this evening."

Halfway to Houston, Billy ran into a terrible thunderstorm. Somewhere near Fort Hood he stopped at a gas station. Attempting to get back on the road in the torrential rain, he pulled out into the path of an 18-wheeler. He and Karen were killed instantly.

When I heard the tragic news, I called Billy's parents. Aunt Loez said "We can hardly stand it, losing them both, but somehow I know they're all right."

I often have lucid dreams, and that night I had one of the most vivid ones ever. I was in the kitchen of Grandma Stewart's old house, sitting at the round table with several other relatives, including both my grandparents. I knew that Grandma and Grandpa and some of the others were no longer in this world, but still I wasn't surprised to see them all there, in a house that had been torn down twenty years ago. All of us were crying, mourning our loss. The door opened and Billy walked in, smiling. He told us, "There's no need to cry. You think I'm dead, but I'm not, I'm still around." I woke up then, still missing my cousin, but feeling comforted.

A few days later, I went to Dublin to be with Billy's family. I told my aunt and uncle about the dream, and how real it felt. They just nodded, not the least bit surprised or skeptical. Aunt Loez told me about the broken air conditioner and Billy's promise to fix it. The day after the accident, she said, all the family had gathered in the living room. As they sat and grieved together, the old machine kept grumbling, feebly attempting to cool the room. Suddenly the noise stopped and the air conditioner began to work perfectly. Sharon looked at her mother, smiling now through her tears. "He said he'd fix it, Mama, and he did!"

Several times in my life, I've had similar lucid dreams about lost loved ones, beginning with my grandmother. She still shows up during stressful times, just to let me know she's watching over me.

> *"There's no need to cry. You think I'm dead, but I'm not, I'm still around."*

I've done meditation off and on for years, and these events happen more often after meditation. I've also experienced psychic moments during meditation, and these have sometimes been somewhat overwhelming. That's when I've stop meditating. Meditation has been helpful to me in so many other ways, especially in "hearing" from friends and family who've passed on, that I've decided it's worth the sometimes-disturbing psychic flashes.

Shirley Wetzel has been a librarian at Rice University for 23 years. She has been a writer for much longer than that, although only recently did she begin writing for publication. She did graduate work in anthropology, participating in archaeological digs in England, Guatemala, and Galveston Island, Texas. Archaeology continues to be a passion. Shirley is currently working on a mystery set in Comanche, Texas. Much of the action takes place at an archaeological site and in a library. Shirley says, "I guess you could say I'm a strong believer in 'write what you know!'"

18. Sassy
Randall H. Loring

O ur family adopted an eight-week-old kitten from a family who hand nursed the litter after the mother cat was killed. We took the tortoise shell (orange, black, and white) tabby cat, which my daughter named Sassy. My whole family liked the kitten but, for some reason, Sassy became attached to me. Even though my wife fed her, and my son and daughter played with her, Sassy always took naps with me in the afternoon before I went to work, and always greeted me when I returned home from work at midnight.

My wife and I always had cats growing up, but never any that had kittens. So, I wanted my family to experience life giving birth up close, albeit with a cat. My mother thought there were enough cats in the world and that I shouldn't allow Sassy to be a mother. A few other people expressed that opinion as well. But the miracle of birth was something I wanted my family to witness. My children were eleven and fifteen at the time, which I thought were good ages. After Sassy was of age, two male cats came a courting. We thought she was pregnant, but never had it confirmed by a vet.

Now, Sassy was never a lap cat or one that liked to be held. You could pet her head and back, but never her belly. One other thing, she never meowed. So one day as I was reading the newspaper in the easy chair, sassy meowed and jumped up onto my lap. I was only able to pet her for a moment before she jumped down and looked at me and started to walk away. I thought her behavior kind of strange but I wanted to get back to reading the newspaper. Less than a minute went by and she jumped back in my lap, jumped down, looked at me and started to walk away. Finally, I got the idea that she wanted something, so I put down the paper and got up. I followed her into my son's room and watched her go into his closet. I was still clueless, because I thought cats gave birth in private. So, still puzzled, I went back to my chair and the newspaper.

Within seconds, the same thing occurred, she was in and out of my lap, and I again followed her back to the closet.

I believe that, when she died, she wanted to let me know that she was all right.

Then, I finally got it! As she walked around in circles in the closet, I knew she was "nesting." I decided to call my wife to see if she could come home for lunch. As I was in the kitchen getting the phone, Sassy showed up and started to meow again so I followed her back to the closet and, at that point, I realized she wanted me to stay with her. While I was lying on the floor, watching, she gave birth to one kitten. My wife arrived to see Sassy licking her new kitten. This occurred on my day off, so I stayed on the floor with Sassy until my daughter came home. It just felt like Sassy wanted me to be there with her all afternoon, so I stayed.

We all went to bed at 10:00 p.m. that night and, since several hours had passed and Sassy hadn't had any more kittens, we thought she was finished. But when my wife got up at 6:00 a.m. the next morning, there were two more kittens in the closet.

Sassy was a good mother, and spent her time with her kittens. After she weaned them, she never ventured far. She would spend her time only on the first floor. We have a cat door that goes out onto our deck so, whenever Mother Nature calls, the cats are free to go outside. I only mention this because Sassy never came upstairs again after giving birth. All her time was usually spent in the dining room, under the table or sitting on the chairs. Of course, if any cat was not around, we just assumed it was outside and would show up at mealtime.

When I get home from work, I arrive around midnight and go right to bed. One night, around 2:00 a.m., I woke up because I had to go to the bathroom. Groggily, I got up and walked around the bed. On the foot of the bed, I noticed a lighted, clear white object. That is what my eyes saw, but I had a knowing inside me that what was on the bed was Sassy. She was on her back looking at me, and I got the most wonderful feeling from her that she was totally blissful. I felt she wanted me to kneel down and pet her, but I had to go to the bathroom first. When I came back to the bedroom, she is gone. I was thinking how strange it was for Sassy to come upstairs and wondered how she could leave the bedroom and walk past the bathroom without me seeing her. Anyway, I went back to bed and thought nothing else of it.

The next day, my wife, Laure, said she hadn't seen Sassy. We didn't think too much about it because it was summer and she could have been outside. After a couple of days, though, Laure said she hadn't even seen Sassy at meal times. Laure was concerned that a wild animal might have gotten Sassy when she went outside. We live in a neighborhood, but woods are only a few houses away.

It is at this point that I remembered Sassy's nighttime visit and I shared my experience with Laure. She got upset, thinking that something could have happened to Sassy. And, she was right. Sassy never did come home. No matter what happened to Sassy, where ever she is, she is totally blissful. I believe that, when she died, she wanted to let me know that she was all right. I had a hard time shedding any tears over losing Sassy. I may feel a loss, but as far as Sassy is concerned, she couldn't be happier.

Randall Loring lives in Bangor, Maine with his wife, Laure, and their two children, Andrew and Victoria. The Lorings are close personal friends the Hoy Family and it was at Randall's urging that the editor of this book, Angela Hoy, further study and explore her own spiritual experiences. This ultimately led to the publication of Real Stories of Spirit Communication, Volumes 1 *and* 2 *and the creation of http://www.SpiritStories.com.*

19. Dad's Dog Tags
Randall H. Loring

W hen my son, Andrew, was about ten, he heard his friends talking about something called the Ouija® board. He asked me about it and I remembered, as a teenager, using one that belonged to my sister's friend. So, I offered to take Andrew to the store and buy one.

Andrew and I brought it home and showed it to my wife and daughter, and then we all took it to his bedroom and attempted to use it. We placed it on our laps and I said, "Anybody out there?"

We had an immediate response of "yes."

At this point, I said, "Do you have a name?"

The answer was "yes."

So I asked what its name was, and it came back with "dad."

My father had passed away about ten years before from a heart attack on a golf course. So, I said to the board, "You're telling me that you are my father?"

The response was "yes."

Now I was thinking, *how can you prove it*? We had just come back from visiting my mother who lives 300 miles away. During our visit, she had given Andrew my father's old "dog tags" from when he'd served in the army during WWII. So I said to the board, "If you are really my father, what were your dog tag numbers?"

I asked my wife to write down the numbers as we got them from the board. After they were written out, we put the board down and I asked my son to see if he could find the dog tags we had brought back home. He found them and we compared the numbers from the tags to what we got from the board. They all matched except for the last two, which were transposed. I later told my older sister about this event and she recalled my father rattling off his numbers once, but he was not sure of the order of the last two digits.

I was convinced my father was indeed communicating with us. So I asked him, "Are you around us?"

He replied, "yes".

I then asked him if he has helped us in any way. His response was "yes" so I asked for an example.

He then said "sledding" After thinking for a moment, I knew what he was talking about. The previous month, my friend, Tom, and I took our kids sledding down a very steep hill. His daughter, who was seven at the time, joined me on my sled and down we went. I couldn't steer very well and we wound up in a groove in the snow that led to a jump that some kids had made. We hit that jump and went airborne. While in the air, all I was thinking was how much it going to hurt and how many bones I was going to break. We then landed and tumbled to a stop. To my amazement, I was able to get up without a scratch on me. My friend's daughter was crying, but was not hurt at all. I mentioned to my friend that I was positive we were going to be injured, and could not explain why we were not.

Unfortunately, using a Ouija® board is time-consuming because the spirit has to spell out every word, unless you think of only yes or no questions. There was not much more I could think of at the time to ask my father, and my son was getting bored, so we put it away.

I am convinced that my father is around, even when I'm not aware of it. If I think of him or if I need any help, he is always there.

Randall Loring's bio appears in the preceding chapter.

20. One Last Goodbye
Diane R. Schmidt

It was a typical Thanksgiving weekend, filled with visiting relatives and shopping for Christmas. I was blissfully happy, knowing that my family was healthy and happy, and Christmas was only a few weeks away. I never suspected that a few days after Thanksgiving I'd receive the most devastating news.

My family and I were getting ready to go to church when the phone rang. This was unusual on a Sunday morning. My husband answered it and handed it to me. It was my mom, telling me my grandmother, her mother, had died in the middle of the night, November 30th. I was in shock. As the news sunk in, I started to cry hysterically. My grandmother had not been ill; she went to her doctor on a regular basis. There was no warning. I had been very close to her, almost like she was a second mother to me. I missed her by two weeks, when I had planned to see her. The last time I had seen her was the previous spring.

I didn't know how to process this news. It seemed unbelievable. I had just received a letter from her and she was so happy and upbeat. She had said she wanted to visit me. This was surprising to me as I lived 10 hours away and we had talked about her visiting, but she never did because it was too long of a trip for her.

I spent the next two weeks in a fog, not believing, not knowing how to handle the news. The Christmas decorations sat in a box on the floor, untouched. Our freshly cut Christmas tree stood in the corner, undecorated. I knew I had to pull myself together, but I didn't know how.

We went to New York as originally planned and visited with everyone, much of the time talking about Grandma and how much we missed her. We visited with Grandpa one evening. This was the hardest visit for me. As we sat in the kitchen, I expected Grandma to come walking up, with a plate of her sugar cookies or

> *I couldn't hear her speaking verbally, but the way she looked at me, she was saying she loved me.*

to tell us a story about the deer in the woods surrounding her house. I kept thinking she was on vacation.

The new year began. Time seemed to help me calm down, but I never felt like I had closure. A few months later, on the 30th of the month, she visited me one last time in a dream.

I dreamt I was standing with her near the edge of the woods, looking at the flowers. For over 60 years, my grandparents had kept gardens filled with flowers and vegetables. One thing we always did when we visited her was look at the gardens. She would tell us about the plants and show us all the wonderful things that were growing. My grandmother was a wonderful gardener.

During the dream, the sun was shining brightly. It was a beautiful day! She was smiling and talking with me. I couldn't hear her speaking verbally, but the way she looked at me, she was saying she loved me. Her eyes sparkled as she spoke and she was so at peace. I never wanted to leave. There were other people there, too, but I couldn't see their faces. I remember thinking in the dream that I was so glad I had this one last time with her and how wonderful it was that she came back to see me. She was so happy and healthy. All of a sudden, I felt myself being pulled away from her. I fought it but woke up, back to this reality. I started hyperventilating when I realized she was gone. This was very unusual, as I have never hyperventilated after a dream. I barely slept the rest of the night. A few days later, I came to realize that this was the closure I needed. She had come to visit me so she could say goodbye and I could have the closure I so desperately needed.

I haven't dreamed of her since, but I think of her often. I know she's around me all the time. I miss her a lot but I'm so grateful I got to see her one last time.

Ohio-based freelance writer Diane Schmidt specializes in copywriting, articles and editing. She has a BA in Communication-Journalism from Marist College and a background in marketing, Internet research and graphic design. She is also owner and editor of http://www.SavingsMania.com.

21. "I Love This Place"
Bradleigh Anne Marshall

D ave and I were great friends, like brother and sister, though it didn't start out that way. When I met him in 1974, I developed a bit of a crush on him. With his long and lean body and long wavy hair, a sweet smile and eyes that laughed, he was a hottie! But I was only 14 and he was 16 and I was just another one of his sister's friends.

Over the course of that first year, we did become closer, but it wasn't until his sister introduced me to the wonders of make-up and styled hair that Dave started looking at me differently. The first time I appeared "done up," he couldn't take his eyes off of me and, for the first time in my life, I felt pretty. He started treating me differently, with more affection I guess, but by then a lot of time had gone by and I really did consider him to be "just a good friend".

By the time he got around to finding the nerve to kiss me, it was too late. We had become so much like brother and sister that it just felt wrong to both of us. So much so that we ended up laughing during the kiss and agreeing that it felt silly. We never tried that again, but our friendship did get a lot deeper.

Dave used to come babysitting with me when I was 15. We'd take care of the kids together and, after they were tucked in for the night, we'd sit on the sofa and talk about everything; our dreams, our goals, our latest crushes, and things like that. One night, he asked me if I believed in ghosts and, after a few minutes of contemplating the truth versus the "yeah right!" option, I admitted I did and shared with him a few of the stories from my long and freaky past. We had a long talk about "spirit communication" that night.

He shared with me a story about his experience when his grandfather passed away. He was with his grandfather when he had a sudden and massive heart attack and, in the moments after his grandfather had grown still on the floor, he told me he heard his grandfather speaking to him. His message was simple; everything was going to be okay. It didn't hurt at all and he felt "light." Dave didn't know what that part meant but he

> *I wanted you to know that news is coming your way. I don't want you to worry. I'm okay.*

told me that he did feel comforted in those awful days afterwards, knowing that "everything was going to be okay."

I told him that it sounded wonderful. I had never known anyone who died and all my communications to that point had come from strangers. I said that if I ever had to know someone who passed away, I hoped they would find a way to let me know that everything would be okay, too. Dave told me that when it happened to him, he'd find a way to let me know. I was 15. He was 17. That day would be decades into our grand futures but I told him that no matter how old we were, I was going to hold him to it.

On July 22, 1979, I went to bed a happy camper and awoke in the morning to a nightmare it took me ages to shake off. Somewhere between the time I fell asleep and dawn I was awakened, I think, to the sound of a familiar voice in my ear. I recognized it immediately and wondered what the hell Dave was doing in my bedroom at that hour. I started to ask but found I couldn't speak. "Listen," he said quietly, "I can't stay but I wanted you to know that news is coming your way. I don't want you to worry. I'm okay. Everything is going to be fine. Love ya!" It felt like he grabbed my toes and gave them a wee shake when he said "love ya."

I looked up at him and smiled, and still unable to really talk I murmured a drowsy "uh huh" and made a mental note to ask him in the morning what was up with the night visit.

At 7:30 a.m., my phone rang and I ignored it. It rang again 15 minutes later and my then-hubby answered it. Moments later, he was standing beside the bed, telling me I had to take the call. Perturbed, I got up and went to the kitchen to take the call.

> *"I'm great! I love this place. It's everything my grandfather tried to tell me it was."*

Nothing in my hubby's demeanor gave it away and I shot him an annoyed look as I plugged in the kettle.

It was my girlfriend, Dave's sister. "I have bad news," she said. "You know my brother, Dave?" she asked as though I might not have. "Of course," I replied. "He's dead." Just like that. No preamble. I thought it was a bad joke and told her so. After all, I had just seen him a few hours ago. He talked to me!

"You couldn't have," she wailed through her tears. "He died last night at 6:30..." and she proceeded to tell me what had happened.

I listened but still wouldn't believe. I saw him. He talked to me. He touched my foot! Later, I asked my husband if the visit had disturbed him...did he wake up? Had he seen and heard him, too? Of course he hadn't. He didn't really know Dave. The message was for me.

Dave told me years before that he would find a way to let me know that "everything was going to be okay" and he had, though truthfully, I didn't believe that anything would ever be okay again. The news of his death derailed my life in ways I couldn't begin to comprehend. Nothing felt "okay" for a long time afterwards.

About a year later, I found comfort finally in what could best be described as a dream visit. Dave came for me in the night and took me to a park. We sat under the trees on a shockingly comfortable bench and he told me that he was happier than he had ever been in life. He said he was confused when it first happened. His grandfather had been there at the accident scene and kept telling him not to worry, that everything was okay and he just needed to believe it. He told me what it had been like for him in those moments afterwards and that he couldn't believe that any of it was happening.

Dave said he and his grandfather had sat by the side of the road for hours that night, long after the scene had been cleared, talking about what would happen next. He said it was deep into the night when he started to believe that everything was going to be okay. I asked if his girlfriend had been there, too, since she died before he did, but he said she wasn't. She had gone off with a woman.

I told him I had a zillion questions to ask him but he told me that what I was seeing and feeling then was all I needed to know. "Stop, look, feel," he said, and I did. I sat quietly beside him on the bench and just allowed myself to be where he was. It was warm and comfortable, and I felt safer than I had ever felt before or since. The air was clean and fresh and the beauty was something to be seen and felt. There was a sense of peace and belonging that I had never known.

"This is what you need to know," he said. I nodded. I was without words. "Feel better?" he asked with a smile. Again I nodded. "Now stop being so sad all the time!" he said. "I'm great! I love this place. It's everything my grandfather tried to tell me it was."

"What is this place?" I asked him. "It's home," he replied. And, for whatever reason, I accepted that answer.

The next morning, I awoke with the sense that a huge weight had been removed from my life. I could think of Dave and smile again. I could think about death and not be terrified because he had found a way to show me that we don't cease to be just because our time on this plane comes to an end. There is something beyond this, something wonderful and real.

I believe now, even in the darkest moments of pain and loss, that there is "light" and that, for our loved ones, "everything will be okay." And for those of who have been treated to these messages, we know, too, that for us, the survivors, "everything *is* okay."

Bradleigh Anne Marshall is a part-time "slice of life" writer and fulltime leisurist who enjoys the written word more than most. A long time believer in the natural and the supernatural, Bradleigh has spent a lifetime looking for, and sharing stories of inspiration. She can be reached at bradleigh.marshall@shaw.ca.

22. Missing
J. Gayle Kretschmer

O ur son, Ken, had gone up to Washington State to see his lifetime friend, Pete, his wife, Mioke, and some of the old gang. He flew back to Reno a day earlier than we expected him and called us to let us know he was back in Nevada. He said he'd be home in a day or two and that he wanted to look into job possibilities with the police department in Reno. He had recently resigned from the Sheriff's Department in Tonopah.

But he never came home.

We began to worry that something was wrong. It wasn't like Ken not to keep us informed of any change in plans. We called his friend, Mark, in the Tonopah Sheriff's Department and asked him to put out a missing person's bulletin on Ken. Mark also drove to Reno to try and locate him, urging us to stay home in case Ken called - a decision I regret to this day.

Thursday night, three days after Ken had told me he'd be home "in a couple of days," I went to bed feeling restless and worried, my mind full of Ken. After a long while, I fell into a deep slumber. Something jerked me awake. It wasn't a noise, it was just…something. I strongly felt a presence in the room. I sat up, opened my eyes, and saw Ken standing in the bedroom, smiling at me. He appeared to be carrying a baby, or something covered with a blanket, in his arms and he walked toward me. I reached out to him, saying, "Ken, you're home, you're okay."

But he ignored my outstretched arms and stepped backwards to the open bedroom door. "Ken," I pleaded, "Please don't go." But he slowly faded away.

I realized then that it was not Ken in the flesh, but his spirit. I knew then I would never see him again. I thought he was dead.

But he wasn't dead–not then.

> *I sat up, opened my eyes, and saw Ken standing in the bedroom, smiling at me.*

Sunday evening, two Tonopah deputies knocked on our door and told us that Ken had been found in a Sparks motel room in bed, and that he was deceased. Our worst fear had happened.

My mind tried to reason, how-why did Ken appear to me on Thursday night–Alive?! It seemed impossible that he could, yet he did.

The only thing that made sense was one of two things: 1) He was there to tell me he needed help, or 2) He was there to say goodbye. Whichever it was, what was the 'thing' he carried? That we will never understand. One theory was that he was carrying his "baby self", that he had come to tell me he had loved me as a baby, and as an adult. But how will I ever know?

According to our doctor, the autopsy done on Ken told us very little. So, we don't even know how Ken died. We suspect he was ill, as did out doctor, and he said Ken could have had an arrhythmia in his heart, which would not show up on an autopsy.

He was found dead in that motel room at 5:30 p.m., and the clerk said he had come into the office that same morning to pay for another day. We'll never know what really happened, and there is so much mystery surrounding his death. Actually, I wondered – feared – it was suicide. But that is one thing the autopsy ruled out. We will never know what really happened, only that our son was gone.

Ken was only thirty-one, much too young to die.

J. Gayle Kretschmer is a grandmother and a writer of novels and freelance features and stories. She lives in Fernley, Nevada with her husband of 49 years.

23. My Ever Watchful Sister
Allen Shaw

I never believed in spirits, ghosts, poltergeists or any other form of life after death. I even had problems with the whole concept of God during my rebellious teenage years. All that came to a crashing halt in college.

During the Fall of 1992, in the midst of my first Hell Week of my first semester in college (the week preceding finals), I had an experience that made me realize I had been a part of this phenomenon my whole life. My sister, Savannah, came to visit me during this week. The problem with this visit? My sister died in 1969.

But, let's start at the beginning. My sister, Savannah, died when she was barely 18-months-old. I was five at the time. After her death, I began dreaming about her on a regular basis. But, as most five-year-olds (and most adults as well), I never remembered the whole of my dreams. I just remembered bits and pieces. I never really gave it much thought until that fateful night studying for a Criminal Justice 101 class.

During that night, while sleeping with my face in a book, slobber drooling all over my notes and a cigarette stub in my fingers, Savannah came to visit once again. This time, I remembered everything in the dream. I knew I was dreaming from the beginning because Savannah was the age she would have been if she lived, but she still had her 18-month-old face. I later realized she did this on purpose because she wanted me to know who she was. Savannah told me she had been coming to me for years. She told me she had been watching me my whole life and her only worry was that I didn't seem to know when I was stressed out. She said she was afraid I was going to get sick. And then she told me to take a break.

After that, the only time I ever dreamed about Savannah was when I was stressed out. She has shown up when I've been working too hard. She has shown up when I haven't had a vacation in a while. She has shown up when I've been confused about a girl I was dating. Every time she visits, she offers advice on how to handle whatever situation I've found myself in. Every single time I've followed her advice, things worked out for the best.

In the last year, she has been coming to me with a different face. She is still the age she would be if she had lived. But now she looks more like my Mom. I asked about the change. My Guardian Angel (as I had come to call her by this time) told me she was no longer worried that I wouldn't recognize her. She said that the first few times she came to me, I ignored whatever advice she had given me and things didn't work out. But now that I believed she was real, there was no need to convince me.

I am still not sure about the existence of ghosts, spirits, poltergeists or any other form of life after death. I still have questions about God. And I am not one of those people who believe that dreams are more than nature's way of sifting through the garbage in our subconscious minds. I can usually determine why I dreamed a certain dream. Usually it has to do with something I saw on TV, read in a book or experienced during my daily life. I am a cynic by nature. Most of the time, I see an ulterior motive in everything. Faith for faith's sake has never been a motto I lived by.

But then Savannah will come to me again. Usually, when Savannah makes her unannounced visits, I haven't given her even a cursory thought in a few months. She talks to me about my life and what I'm doing wrong. And more importantly, what I'm doing right. And she's always able to make me remember the whole of the "dream" she has starred in, which is something I still don't do with my regular, day-to-day dreams. And when I follow her advice, my life always seems to work out for the better.

This experience has done nothing to deter my cynical nature in most aspects of my life. But it has made me realize I am not as smart as I once thought I was. It has made me realize that questions are good. Don't accept anything at face value. And the most important lesson it has taught me is this: just because I can't see it, touch it, smell it or argue with it doesn't mean it doesn't exist. And sometimes, that's a good thing.

Allen Shaw is a burgeoning freelance writer and the current news director at USA News Network. He writes a daily eight- to nine-page newscast for college radio around the country. Not only is he the news director, but he's also the sole reporter, movie critic and music connoisseur. Examples of his movie and music reviews can be found at online at http://www.usanewsnetwork.com and http://www.catskilleagle.com.

24. Frank's Story
Christine Cristiano

In August 2001, my father, Frank Pupillo, passed away unexpectedly at the age of sixty-six. He'd been complaining of ill health for a few weeks but the blood tests ordered by his doctor revealed nothing. Ironically, my brother-in-law had been diagnosed with cancer a few months earlier and wasn't expected to survive beyond six months. My sister was living out of the country and my parents were spending weeks at a time at my sister's place trying to help out.

One hot Wednesday evening, my mother called to tell me that my father was in severe pain. I drove over to their home and accompanied my mother to the nearest hospital. I had seen my father a few days earlier but, in a very short time, his health had deteriorated rapidly. His skin was an ashen color and he needed help getting into the car. After spending a night in the emergency ward, he was diagnosed with acute leukemia the following morning. Due to his severe condition, the doctor felt a transfer to a larger cancer center in the city was his best chance for survival.

There was no room in the ambulance to let my mother accompany my father to the cancer center, so we had reassured him that we would meet him at the cancer center when he arrived.

My father called later that day and said the transfer was slightly delayed and he would call us when he got there. Around seven that evening, my father called again to let us know that he had finally arrived. He suggested that we wait until morning to come to the hospital because the attending doctor was going to send him for more tests. The last time my mother spoke with him was around ten o'clock that evening. At five o'clock the next morning, we received a call from the hospital informing us that he had a stroke. My mother and I rushed to the hospital, which was about an hour away, but he had already passed before we arrived.

It had been only thirty-six hours since he had first been admitted to the hospital. Regrettably, we didn't have the chance to inform anyone that he was ill and hospitalized. At his time of passing, one of my sisters was away on vacation, my other sister was living out of the country, and my brother lived over an hour away. It was now up to my mother, my husband, and me to call everyone and announce my father's passing.

Immediately upon his passing, my home was bombarded by monarch butterflies. What made this occurrence so strange was that monarch butterflies were virtually nonexistent around my house. At the time, I was living in a new housing development and the area lacked any trees and flowers due to the ongoing construction.

That evening, after returning from the hospital, a neighbor had dropped by to offer her condolences. As we were sitting quietly on my porch, four monarch butterflies suddenly appeared and started to flutter around us. Their unexpected visitation lasted for about fifteen minutes. My neighbor remarked how strange it was that to see monarch butterflies around my house.

On the day of my father's funeral, my oldest son wanted to attend the service. I had arranged for my neighbor to bring him to the church because I had to go to the funeral home first. When I arrived at the church, my neighbor and my son were standing on the church steps. My neighbor informed me that, upon their arrival, a pure, white butterfly had flickered gracefully around my son for quite some time. When my son put his hand out, the butterfly hovered over it.

After the ceremony, the immediate family was in the parking lot behind the church, loading up the cars with all the flowers and tributes. As the adults were busy packing up, the grandchildren were standing in a circle waiting to leave. My son was emotionally drained and took a seat on the cement curb a few feet away. Out of the blue, a monarch butterfly appeared and proceeded to flicker softly around the group of children. The monarch butterfly then floated over to where my son was sitting and began to encircle him in its flight.

About a month after my father's passing, I accompanied my mother to take care of some legal matters. We were close to my house and decided to stop in for lunch. After lunch, we took our tea and sat outside on the porch, enjoying the cool September air. Much to our delight, a monarch butterfly flitted onto the porch and proceeded to flutter around my mother for quite some time. This visitation was particularly strange because we hadn't witnessed the butterflies since the day of my father's funeral. To this day, I had never seen monarch butterflies around my house or in my yard.

Months later, my sister, mother, and I were still reeling over my father's and my brother-in-law's passing. A friend of ours volunteered the contact number for a psychic that she had seen after the passing of her father and mother. We decided to book an appointment with the psychic to see if we could gain some closure and contact my father. When we arrived at our appointment, my mother didn't tell the psychic why we had come. Immediately, the psychic confirmed that my father had passed and was here with us. She told us that my father was enjoying a brandy with his friends and was fine. Ironically, expensive brandy was my father's alcoholic beverage of choice. The psychic went on to relate details about my father that she couldn't possibly have known. My father was a joker and was always the life of the party; somehow the psychic had captured that sense of him. At one point during our session, she started laughing and commented that my father was telling her that he was just as surprised to find himself dead as we were. This is definitely something my father would have said! After the conclusion of my session with the psychic, I experienced a profound sense of peace that he was well, not alone and had been reunited with relatives and friends who had passed.

It's been three years since my father's sudden passing. We have seen the psychic again and have been in contact with my father. The psychic always relates something new that my father has observed in our lives, thus giving us proof that he is still among us. He is usually flocked by other relatives that have passed, including, most recently, my cousin who passed away a few months ago. Surprisingly, his constant companion, who appears with our sessions, is my husband's father, Vincent, who passed away thirty years ago, when my husband was a very young boy.

> *This visitation was particularly strange because we hadn't witnessed the butterflies since the day of my father's funeral.*

Since his passing and the appearance of the monarch butterflies, my new home is now adorned with trees, shrubs and flowers but I have never been visited by a monarch butterfly again, despite my efforts to attract them with ornate butterfly-attracting flowers.

If someone had asked me before my father's passing if I believed that our loved ones could contact us from the other side, I probably would've said no. I do remember my father and sister joking around and promising that whoever went first would come back to let us know that they were still here in spirit. My father kept his promise and we were able to find peace with his passing.

Christine Cristiano hangs her hat in Ontario, Canada. Her work has appeared in numerous print and online venues in the U.S. and Canada.

25. Turquoise Bird Stinkie
Anna Teague

W hen I was in the fourth grade, I had dozens of pet chickens, scratching and pecking up all the grass in our backyard. Okay, let's just say enough chickens to wreak havoc on my Dad's dream of a gorgeous, poop-free lawn. "Sell them," my parents exclaimed, "And you can take the money and buy a parakeet."

"A parakeet!" I cried, "But, I love my chickens!" Mom and Dad, I must say, have to get an A-plus for effort. They didn't give up.

"A parakeet is smaller and much easier to take care of. They're cute and loving. Besides, we already have a buyer for the chickens." I guess I was convinced. Reluctantly, I watched my chickens get loaded up and driven away by some lady. Saying goodbye was hard.

My parents took me to the local pet store so I could pick out a baby parakeet to take home. Behind a sheet of glass windows with a wooden door on one side, there were lots of baby parakeets. I chose a beautiful turquoise bird which I called Stinkie, short for Stinker.

For fourteen years, Stinkie slept beside my bed and woke me with sweet melodies the minute she saw me move. One evening, while I was away, my little bird passed on after a tragic battle with an illness. My world collapsed. Memories and guilt for not being with Stinkie at the end cut me apart. I knew I had done everything I could for her the last few months of her life. Why couldn't the medicine have worked?

Over and over, I kept remembering. I had never felt this kind of pain before. It was unbearable. No one could offer me comfort. On the fourth day of my mourning cries, while I was sitting in my room, I found myself calling, "Stinkie, Stinkie, I miss you. Come home." A quiet singing came from behind me and there, on top of the door, was Stinkie, plain as the nose on my face. I rubbed my eyes and blinked. She was gone. "Stinkie," I called. Nothing.

Later that evening I called again. "Stinkie." I caught sight of her sitting on my bed, but only briefly. For a week, Stinkie appeared shortly after I called. There was one instance where I reached my hand out to her and she stepped into it like she had always done. I lifted my hand up to my face. We looked into each other's

> *Being as fragile as my heart was during that period in my life, I found great comfort in knowing my baby bird was okay and lived on.*

eyes and she disappeared. Warmth, comfort and love filled my entire being.

Being as fragile as my heart was during that period in my life, I found great comfort in knowing my baby bird was okay and lived on. I take comfort in knowing my love for her and her love for me will always exist forever, growing endlessly until the time comes when we will be reunited.

I love you, Stinkie.

Born in Texas, Anna Teague enjoys writing and the friendship and love of her Conure bird. They are dear friends that continue growing together. She would love to find a cure-all for diseases, which makes herbals and vitamins among her passions. Anna believes they are one of the keys to lasting health.

26. Uncle Ronnie
Pamela Drummond

U ncle Ronnie wasn't really my uncle. He was just a friend of the family who was head-over-heels in love with my mother. It was the Summer of 1973. My parents' divorce had been final for several months and my mother, my sister, and I were still adjusting to our new truncated life without my father. Uncle Ronnie had been a friend of my parents for years, but even though my sister and I were only high school age, we could always tell that Ronnie was smitten with my mother. He always brought her plants on her birthday, Mother's Day, Thanksgiving, Christmas -- basically any excuse he could find, because he knew she loved plants and had an extensive garden in the atrium of our home.

Our house was shaped like a large letter I. The living room, kitchen, dining room and den made up the top of the I, the hallway and two bedrooms made up the shaft of the I, and my mother's room, the bathroom, the laundry room and the garage made up the base of the I. The atrium was a lattice topped area made up of three walls of the house: the wall with the front door leading into the living room, a wall of windows that lined the hall, and a wall with a sliding glass door that lead to the laundry room.

After my parents' divorce, Uncle Ronnie could be found most days doing work in the atrium or other odd jobs around the house. He never professed his love for my mother, I don't know if he respected my father too much or if he just didn't want to do it too soon after the divorce, but he showed us his feelings in hundreds of tiny ways.

One Friday night, my mother wasn't feeling well, so she went to bed early. My sister and I stayed up watching TV in the den. Suddenly, a chill filled the air, and we heard something in the back of the house. The hair rose on our arms and we looked at each other with wide eyes. We grabbed a rolling pin from the kitchen and went to investigate. When we reached the head of the hallway, we saw a dark figure through the billowing curtains of the hall windows. The figure was walking from the laundry

> *He touched her foot and then he turned and left through the open sliding glass door in her bedroom.*

room toward our mother's bedroom. We froze in terror until the figure turned his face toward us and we recognized Uncle Ronnie. He smiled at us and nodded and proceeded to our mother's room. It was strange that he would be in the house that late at night, but we figured our mother must have called him over for something.

The next morning, we asked our mother about his visit. Her face went pale. She said that she'd thought it was a dream. She had woken and found Uncle Ronnie standing at the foot of her bed, just looking at her. She asked him what he was doing there, but he simply gave her a melancholy look. She told him he was scaring her. He touched her foot and then he turned and left through the open sliding glass door in her bedroom.

Now that she knew it wasn't a dream, she called his house to ask him what he'd been doing, but she got no answer. Later that day, a neighbor came over and asked if we'd heard the latest news. Ronnie had been found dead a few hours before in his house. It was presumed to be a heart attack, and from the state of the body, he'd been dead at least two days.

We went over the incident from the night before and realized that Uncle Ronnie had been dead at least a day and the hall windows had been closed, but we had seen Uncle Ronnie at the end of the hall through the billowing hall window curtains. Chills ran down our spines but we weren't afraid. Somehow we knew it was just Uncle Ronnie saying his last goodbyes.

Pamela Drummond is an aspiring writer who lives in Southern California with her husband, Bob, her son, James, and her cats Six-Pack (six toes on each foot) and Cow Kitty (spotted like a Jersey cow). Several strange incidents in her life, including the sighting of Uncle Ronnie and her own death for 90 seconds while delivering her son James, have given her an interest in the paranormal. Through the two incidents mentioned above, she's learned to not fear death and to respect the paranormal as a reality. She writes paranormal suspense with one of her finished novels based loosely on her own after-death experience.

27. Love Never Dies
T. D. Phillips

J im was like my Dad and he treated me as his daughter, even though he was just my uncle, my favorite uncle. We were very close, and have always had a very special bond between us. He always sheltered me from the trouble that was going on.

When Jim was murdered on January 11, 1981, I was completely devastated. Less than three days later, the first day back to school for me, I was sitting in the band room and I suddenly felt him behind me, laying a hand on my shoulder. I turned around, saying, "Jim?" But he wasn't there. My deep grief had been alleviated by his presence. My friend, Sheila, was sitting right beside me when this happened. The hairs on her entire body stood up and she also felt his presence.

That wasn't the only communication I have had with Jim. I began to see him everywhere I looked for a long time. In automobiles, at restaurants, everywhere! He even physically manifested in my doctor's office when I was ill with the flu. He was dressed in the suit that he was buried in and, as he came through that door, he looked at me and smiled. His craggy face was warm and aglow with love. There were no marks other than the scars on his face. He was trying to tell me that all was going to be okay. Then he turned and walked out the door.

In 1991, I was engaged to be married but didn't know that the young man that I was about to marry was a drug dealer and a drug user. Jimmy had been killed in a drug-related setup in 1981. Unknown to me, my impending marriage was a violation of the promise that I'd made to Jimmy during Christmas of 1980, that I would never get involved with the Mob or drugs. One night, as a drug dealer that my fiancé brought with him came into the house, I could hear Jim's voice going from a whisper to a scream, saying, "Get the hell out of there!" I heard it for a little over five minutes

> *I could hear Jim's voice going from a whisper to a scream, saying, "Get the hell out of there!"*

and it didn't stop. His voice kept coming back for about three weeks and I finally left my fiancé and moved back home.

Now, I feel Jim's hands on my shoulders whenever I am down or hurting. Recently, I have been able to communicate with his spirit. During one of those times, he finally asked me to call him Dad. There has been another time, when the case into his death was reopened. Jimmy told me flat out that the truth would be known, that we would see it in the reenactment. We did, and are currently working to reopen his case after 25 years. He showed me how he died, but I cannot prove it in a court of law. I feel his presence by my side even now as I type these words.

T. D. Phillips has been writing poetry for 20 years.

28. Protector
T. D. Phillips

I was very close to my beloved Grandmother Phillips. When she died, I was devastated. Not long after she died, I woke up one night hearing her call my name, and I answered her. She appeared as real as life and sat down on the bed. We talked about several very painful issues in regards to my father, meaning Dad's homosexuality, his abuse of me, and other things. At that point, she did not mention any trouble. My heart healed as the conversation continued. Then she vanished.

I woke up one other morning and had just come into the living room of my apartment when I saw Grandmother standing at the east window. She appeared solidly real. She looked at me with a look of warning. I knew that something was very wrong but I didn't know what. Later that day, while I was visiting my dad in prison, he went ballistic, verbally and physically attacking me for something that my mother had asked me to do. After that incident, my grandmother appeared to my mother and told her exactly what had happened to me. Needless to say, Mom was on the next plane home.

Grandmother has appeared to me countless times to comfort me and to warn me when something was wrong. I hear her voice in my mind and it comforts me when I am down. I am blessed that we continue to talk. She is indeed my protector.

T.D.'s bio appears in the preceding chapter.

29. Just a Breath Away
J. M. Cornwell

Over the years, one stroke after another took my grandmother, Lottie May, away, inch-by-inch. She changed from a vibrant, sassy, intelligent, and loving woman into a shell that resembled her but whose eyes lacked the sparkle and simple joy of life. And, as this change occurred, I went to see her less and less often. It's hard to lose someone in a senseless accident or even after a protracted illness, but to watch the lighthouse of their mind dim slowly is worse.

Strokes took my grandmother's physical functions first and each succeeding stroke took a little more of her mind, until her body was changed into a tightening fetal ball that could not be straightened. Even the gentlest and most loving touch tore her fragile skin and brought screams of pain. During the six years my grandmother existed in the nursing home, my mother went every evening to see her, to sit and talk with her. Age-dimmed blue eyes looked back at us with no recognition, on her face the smile of an infant to whom our faces and voices were a soft blur of colors and sounds.

The strokes continued to kill half of her brain and the doctors intervened time and again with tubes and medication, cutting holes in her body to force feed her and keep her alive a little longer. Finally, when her body could take no more of their interventions, the doctors decided to take my grandmother off all the machines and let her die. I was asked if I wanted to be there and decided I couldn't face watching the death of the only grandmother I ever knew, like some circus attraction. I stayed home and cried, unsure if I had made the right decision or if I was being selfish and disrespectful.

My mother called later that afternoon to tell me my grandmother was gone and had slipped away peacefully. But I had let her go many months before, when she no longer recognized any of us. I felt that what had died that afternoon was the shell of my grandmother, not the woman with whom I spent so many happy afternoons together, laughing and talking and cooking. I clung to those moments like a drowning woman clinging to a bit of wreckage in a storm-wracked sea.

> *I'll always be just a prayer away.*

I went to bed early that night, worn out from crying and unable to concentrate long enough to do anything productive. I tossed and turned, tried to read, and finally, a little after midnight by the nightstand clock, I fell asleep.

I don't remember any dreams. What I do remember is a light burning brighter and brighter against my eyelids. I sat up on the side of the bed, thinking I had forgotten to turn out the hall light, and went to the bedroom door. Groggily, I fumbled to open the door wider, reaching around the doorframe for the light, but it was off. I flipped the switch on and then off again, but the light persisted. I walked into the hall and saw a figured dressed in blue. It was my grandmother. She was wearing her favorite ankle length, smocked blue robe with the quilted Mandarin collar. Shining with a soft white light, she stood there as if waiting for me to recognize her.

I couldn't stop the tears running down my cheeks as I reached out to her. She took my hands and held me closely, my chin grazing the soft halo of her silver hair, and patted my back while I cried.

"I'm sorry," I said between sobs," but I couldn't stand to be there today. I just couldn't watch."

"It's all right," she murmured. "I knew you were there for me, even if you weren't in the room. It's all right."

Still holding her hands, I stepped back, and looked down at her as she smiled up at me. I didn't know what to say and I didn't want to let her go, but I knew I must, just as I had let her go when she no longer recognized me and I knew she wasn't coming back.

"I wanted to tell you something," she said. "I have always believed in you even though you don't believe in yourself. Believe in yourself and follow your heart and remember I'll always be just a prayer away." And then she was gone.

When I woke the next morning, I wasn't sure at first if I had dreamed my grandmother was standing in the hall or if it had been real, but it didn't matter. I still felt her around me.

I went to the funeral three days later and went up to the coffin, not because it was expected but because I wanted to touch her one last time. Her body was straight again and she wore her favorite blue dress. I touched her cold cheek, but I knew she wasn't lying in that box. She was just a prayer away.

J. M. Cornwell is a nationally syndicated journalist, security columnist, author, professional editor with 28 years of experience, prose editor and chief webmaster for The Rose & Thorn *literary ezine. She writes* Grammar Goofs, *a column on grammar, for* Scribe & Quill, Occam's Razor, *a paranormal column, for* Whim's Place, *edits erotica and mystery/suspense novels for* Another Chapter *and runs* Creative Ink, LLC, *a professional editing service. Visit her blog on Blogger.com.*

30. A Life-Saving Umbrella
Celia Sue Hecht

M y father, Argo Irving Hecht, died on April 5, 1987. I found him in bed that morning. His lifeless body made it obvious that he had passed over. The night before and the previous 90 days had been tough. Dad's last days began when he had a mild heart attack and, initially, he seemed to recover quickly. He'd had a heart condition since I was 13 years old so I was relieved at his quick recovery. But soon, his condition worsened until he was given emergency bypass surgery after his lungs had filled up with fluids.

It was painful letting go, and having our roles reversed, but we were clearing up misunderstandings and I experienced many healings. For the first time in my life, he told me how proud he was of me and hugged me for a long while in a way that he had never done before. This was a miracle to me.

The night before he passed, I woke up in the middle of the night when I heard my parents in distress. Apparently, my father's feet were paralyzed, and he could not move. His wife was trying to help him go into the bathroom. But his feet weren't going anywhere. In a crazy fit of rage, I asked in the name of Jesus for help and commanded dad's feet to walk. Okay, so maybe I had read too many bible stories. But unbelievably, it worked, to our astonishment! He was then able to walk to the bathroom of his own volition.

At that point, I realized something was terribly, terribly wrong but I could not admit to myself that my father was dying. I spent the night in prayer and kept checking in on him. Finally, the last time I went in, I realized he was gone. I spent the next few months in shock over his passing. Within a week, I was in England. While there, I kept feeling my dad's presence around me. It seemed as though he was walking with me and trying to communicate. I felt numb because my whole world seemed completely awry without

> *We danced together in a celebration of joy and reunion.*

him. My anchor and sense of security were gone. I didn't know what to do without him and I felt angrier than I had ever felt before. It just wasn't fair that he was gone.

For the next few years, I traveled around the world with a prayer ministry that prayed for others (intercessory prayer). I often, coincidentally, found myself praying with and for people who had just lost their father. Eventually, I experienced a whole new sense of security within myself, and my faith and trust in the divine grew strong. Since Dad was gone, I now had to take care of myself in ways I had never had to do before and somehow the world seemed a more benevolent place to live in.

Sometimes, I tried to talk to him, although I didn't really believe that he could hear me. One time, a holy man told me that he had a message for me from my dad. It was a message of hope, but I was still skeptical about communicating with someone who had gone to the Great Beyond. At the time, I was struggling with my beliefs about death. Growing up, I had come to believe that when a person died, they just went, ashes to ashes, dust to dust, with no afterlife, but I was now considering the possibility that there may be a Heaven or somewhere else to go.

Fast forward nine years. It was now 1996. I had thought the story of Job in the Bible wasn't real until I became him. I was going through a painful divorce, three favorite family members passed away (leaving me an orphan), I lost my job, was rear-ended in a car accident, lost my two cats of five years, and ultimately was diagnosed with fibromyalgia, a chronic pain condition that affections millions of Americans. I am still thankful that no locusts or plagues found me during that dark night of my soul.

During the height of my despair, Dad visited me in a dream one night. The dream began on my old college campus in Florida. I was walking down a hallway and it began to rain. I panicked as if the world was coming to an end because I didn't have an umbrella. I was going to get wet, Heaven forbid, and this seemed overwhelming. But in a twinkling, there was Dad, coming towards me. His hands were outstretched and he was holding a life-saving umbrella. This may seem really trivial, but I felt internally as if he was totally there for me, as if he had never gone away. I still had a savior, my knight in shining armor, after all. We danced together in a celebration of joy and reunion. I knew that he loved me and that he would always be there to protect and guide me. My world that had felt so upside-down became right side up again. I was safe, secure and loved again.

The dream seemed very real as if I had really been with my dad, as if he was still alive. I woke up in wonder at the vivid reality. I was grateful for this miracle, which gave me a bright spot of hope to get me through the gloomy days.

Celia Sue Hecht spins words into bottom line profits... As a published writer, editor, author, and publicist for over 20 years, she has written hundreds of articles for numerous magazines, newspapers and newsletters and obtained media coverage and interviews in all media (radio, TV and print) including LA Times, NY Times, Washington Post, Wall Street Journal, SF Chronicle, Marin Independent Journal, Nevada Business Journal, Nevada Woman, Real Woman magazine, Reno Gazette Journal, NPR, ABC, CBS and NBC affiliates, locally and nationally. Call 888-260-4673 or visit her website at http://www.Write4U.website-by-you.com/page/page/1188499.htm.

31. A Rose by Any Other Name
Celia Sue Hecht

I had never seen anyone communicate with the dead before but here was this guy on television (The Larry King Show) who was doing just that. His name was John Edward and he was giving audience members messages from their loved ones who had crossed over. At first, I was skeptical, but continued to watch, listen, and learn. I have always tried to be open-minded even though I am a born and bred New Yorker at heart (it helped that so is John Edward and that he grew up in close proximity to where I did).

A few years before, while doing a meditation at a seminar, I had been shown that my first name, Celia (that I never really called myself), was more meaningful than I knew and held clues to my true identity. Besides, it was divinely inspired, whereas I had always considered it a big mistake. The only time I had been called Celia in junior high school, the kids had teased me mercilessly.

The family storyline goes that I was named after my paternal grandmother, who had died before I was born. My father, Argo Irving, was very close to his mother and was devastated when she passed while he was overseas fighting in World War II. He jumped ship and went AWOL to attend her funeral. Whenever anyone called me Celia when I was a baby, he cried. Of course, no one could stand seeing a grown man cry, so they stopped calling me by her name and I grew up knowing myself only as Susan (my middle name)...that is, until my first day in kindergarten. The teacher called me this foreign name (Celia) that I couldn't remember hearing before. I ran home crying and found out that I had been given a family legacy of which I had formerly been blissfully unaware. My two cousins were also named for this saintly grandmother, but they were given derivatives of the name (Alice and Civia).

As I watched John Edward talking to people and giving them messages from the beyond, I felt an unusual presence who began talking to me. She introduced herself as Celia, my late grandmother. I

> *The only way to describe the communication was that she was talking to me inside of my head.*

didn't see her but the only way to describe the communication was that she was talking to me inside of my head.

She explained that the reason she had come to visit with me was that I had to know about my name, that it wasn't a fluke, but a clue to my spiritual heritage. She asked me about my two cousins and I realized for the first time that I was the only one who had been given her true name. She told me that this was divinely conceived and it was important for me to know that my first name was not a mistake. She seemed very real and we had a connection that death could not sever.

I enjoyed talking with her and I grew to understand that I am not alone, have never been alone, and would never be alone ever again. There were people on the other side looking out for me and they always would.

A few years later, I shared this story with one of my dearest friends and spiritual teachers, who helped me define my name still further. We looked it up. Ultimately, Celia means celestial, heavenly being. This clue is still somewhat overwhelming for me to identify with, but I am a work in progress.

Celia Sue Hecht's bio appears in the preceding chapter.

32. Guardian Angel Mom
Pamela White

In 1998, my new husband and I moved into a pre-civil war home in a small New York village. We'd looked for months to find a house we agreed on. The first miracle was that my children adored the house at first sight, picked their bedrooms and decreed the house was ours. The second miracle was who apparently moved in with us.

It was only a few months after moving in that we smelled the cigar smoke in the living room. We checked the outlets, oven, cellar and attic but nothing was hot. In fact, the smoke smell never moved from the doorway between the living room and dining room. After ten minutes it disappeared. We joked about the "smoking man" and whispered about ghosts when the children were not around.

I wrote an essay about the smoking man and entered it in a writing contest for which I was awarded an honorable mention. We still thought we were joking about ghosts, but during the day when I was alone, I would walk up stairs and be greeted by the scent of lily of the valleys. I loved the scent and only recognized it because it was the scent my mother used. We nicknamed the bearer of the scent "Lily" and began to share information about when and where Lily and the Smoking Man would appear, or rather where their scents would appear.

At the same time, I was writing my way through several short mystery rejections. I started a story about a psychic who was well on her way to solving a murder. I just needed a way to make the psychic's messages ring true, or that was what I told myself when I drove to a nearby spirit message circle one night. I expected to find oddball people in black capes but was greeted by middle-aged women in sweatshirts and jeans. I felt right at home.

The circle started and I worked hard to memorize all the comments and buzzwords: "He just wants to be acknowledged," "You may think this doesn't mean anything, but I promise that tomorrow you'll realize what the message means." The spirits were also practical, directing a woman where to find her grandmother's missing heirloom earrings, and providing a desired sour cream and peach crumble pie recipe for another circle attendee. Great details to add to the story, I thought.

Two of the women brought a female spirit through, shared that her name was Jan, and described her. They said she was there for me and that she was saying she was my mother. They went on to talk about the lily she was holding and that she came through with her father to teach me something I needed to know.

These women had never met me before, so I was breathless at the details they provided. What shocked me most was that my mother was with her father, her tormenter, abuser, and molester, and whom she never saw after she was 12 years old. I understood the lesson of forgiveness she was bringing through, the idea that forgiveness beyond the physical world is complete, without exception, nearly incomprehensible.

The two mediums told me that she was keeping her promise to look after my children. They told me to look for signs that she was around and to talk to her. Her closing statement was that it was time for me to give her more attention, that the smoking man had already had his turn, apparently a reference to my honorable-mention essay about him. I couldn't help laughing.

I didn't sleep that night, thinking over our odd experiences in the house. I added up the footsteps that walked back and forth in the upstairs hall (old houses creak, don't they?), all the missing things, pennies dropped on the floor leading through the house, lost keys and found glasses. The last thing I was counseled by the message circle women to do was to look for a yellow flower. I shrugged it off, forgiving their error. It was still March and the snow was six inches deep on the ground.

Two days later, I looked out my office window and there, in the front flowerbed, a lone yellow daffodil had broken through the snow.

> *She appeared not to see me, but the older female in the passenger seat sure did. She leaned forward and looked at me, smiling this wickedly outrageous grin.*

On another morning, my younger daughter asked if I believed in ghosts, then proceeded to tell me about the night before. "I was lying in bed and woke up to footsteps in the hall. A woman walked by my door. At first, I thought it was you, Mom, but I realized that she was walking toward the wall, and never came back." She insisted the woman looked like me. She also insisted I do something about it. I stopped feeling inhibited, and started talking to my mother during the day, asking her to be careful about showing herself to the children, that I needed her help watching over them, that I was beginning to remember good things about our difficult relationship.

Somehow, without seeing her myself (although we were seeing others periodically moving through the hallways or on the back porch), I felt comforted during tough times and mothered when lonely. One night, while having a flare-up of my fribromyalgia, I woke screaming from pain coming from my shoulder. My husband jumped up and went to get me a pain pill while I tried to calm down. I felt a warm hand on my shoulder and heard a soft 'shhh' and fell immediately into a pain-free sleep. My husband returned to find me quiet and dozing, to his relief.

I did go back to the message circle every four months or so, to try to develop my own psychic abilities, wanting to have a closer connection with spirits and angels. During this time, my eldest, a new driver, went on a school trip to camp. The day they returned, the bus she was on made it back two hours faster than the bus with their suitcases and sleeping bags. She went to her boyfriend's to hang out until the second bus came in. After a few hours had passed, I called his house looking for her. He told me that she'd left thirty minutes before to pick up her stuff, and was on her way home. I waited awhile, then drove down the street to see if she'd had a problem with her car.

About one mile down the road, I saw her approaching in her little blue car. She appeared not to see me, but the older female in the passenger seat sure did. She leaned forward and looked at me, smiling this wickedly outrageous grin. I didn't recognize her, and just watched them drive by. I went a bit further then turned around and followed her back to the house.

"Hey, baby. Who was that woman you were taking home?" I tossed out to her as I walked into the kitchen.

In her annoyed teenage attitude, she made a face, and said, "I didn't give anyone a ride."

"But the woman in your car...I saw her."

"Wro-ong...." and she was off to call her boyfriend about that night's date.

The woman was 50 with brown hair, big black sunglasses and looked...like me.

I told only my husband my suspicions that the passenger was my mother, gone for 15 years, and we were both comforted. I went back to the message circle but never said a thing. One of my favorite women there turned to me and asked who had the new car. "My daughter," I said. "She's a new driver and her father bought her a little car to drive between his house and mine."

"Well," she said, "you sure don't have to worry about her. She never drives alone. Your mother is here, and she's telling you that she sure likes the view from the passenger seat."

When the veil is lifted between the physical and the spirit world, we get a glimpse of hope, love, and forgiveness. If we're truly fortunate, we get to see who is watching over us, loving us, and keeping us safe.

Pam White is the mother of three, a freelance writer, and writing teacher. Her website is at http://www.food-writing.com.

33. Lightning
Janine Peterson

I graduated from high school surrounded by his family, including three uncles, an aunt, their families, and my grandmother. They all stayed in our house for the long weekend celebration. My grandmother was delighted to see her oldest grandchild graduate from high school. My grandfather had passed away unexpectedly when I was only a year old. I was the only grandchild he met while still alive. The spirit of my grandfather saved my life.

That night, after the family left, lightning struck my house. The time was 11:11 p.m. CRACK! I was startled awake. I sat up in bed, staring at the door. Silence echoed, loud after the loud noise. I got out of bed, wearing flannel pants and a t-shirt. I moved quietly, but I didn't know why.

My room was on the top floor at the end of a hall; at the other end of the hall was a closed door. An uncle had slept behind that door with his wife and their two babies. The room was now empty. I didn't know that behind that door, the room was smoldering, the attached attic was filling with smoke. I didn't know the roof was burning and the smoke alarms were shorted out by the lightning. Had I opened the door, I might have created a back draft, consuming the room, the walls, the draperies, and me.

I walked toward the door, intending to investigate the noise and the odd smell in the air. I would open the door. I would see the guest room with the sheets and towels my mother had already washed. I would see the door leading into the attic that held my old school papers, our luggage, and my brother's old toys. I would no longer be afraid.

As I walked, a figure appeared at the top of the stairs, between the fire and me. He was gray, indistinct. I knew him immediately as my grandfather.

"Don't go in there," he told me, though he didn't speak. We stared at each other. He didn't back down. Terrified, I ran back to my bedroom and dove under the covers. Eventually I fell back asleep.

"Don't go in there," he told me, though he didn't speak. We stared at each other. He didn't back down.

Our dogs were restless and finally woke my parents. My father smelled smoke, called the fire department, and evacuated everyone. By the time the flames were doused, the sun was rising. Most of the roof was gone. Every room reeked of smoke. Every surface in my bedroom was covered in a fine layer of oily soot. Our luggage melted. My blackened school papers were blowing in the wind and catching on shrubbery. But the flames stayed contained in the attic and in the guest room, only starting to creep down the hall when the firefighters arrived. We all survived. I didn't open the door and spread the flames. My grandfather told me not to.

I keep a photograph of my grandfather on my bookshelf. I pester family for details of his life story. It's the least I can do.

Janine Peterson writes from DC, near where her grandfather used to live. She went to Georgetown University, where he studied. Now, she works as a behavioral science research assistant and sometimes she watches movies at the theater where her grandparents courted.

34. Return of the Ex-Husband
Jenny Durbin

T he last person, living or dead, I expected to encounter in this house was my ex-husband, Larry. This is my first house. I bought it two years after Larry died, fourteen years almost to the day of our divorce. Together we had one son, Adrian, and apparently enough pent up rage to raise the dead.

We argued over the same superficial issues all divorced couples do: who pays for school pictures and orthodontia, whose opinion counts when choosing a day camp versus a babysitter, and who decides what the divorce decree really means by the phrase "reasonable visitation." Our battles looked ferocious, two righteous beasts butting heads. Our grumblings looked fierce and mean and serious. It had to; how else to stay the course and avoid the really treacherous battlefield of who ruined whose life more?

But after enough time went by, like most divorced couples, we eventually settled down to not-quite-so-open hostility. It would be too much to say we had become good friends, but we were getting there. We had moved on with our lives to where we could interact calmly and even pass one another in a school gymnasium without threat of bodily harm, like nodding acquaintances. Ours was a thin veneer of polite civility over a shallow grave of rage.

And then one spring evening a phone call came that caused my blood to run cold and changed Adrian's life in ways he may never guess. "At 5:30 this evening," began a controlled voice I didn't know on the other end of the line, "a traffic accident on Beechmont Avenue involved a van and a motorcycle. Larry was killed." It is the sort of news that turns your blood to ice water and makes your knees wobble.

I tell you this so you will know that on that Sunday evening when I stood in the dining room of my recently purchased house figuring the complexities of a dress pattern, I was as surprised as

112

anyone that Larry was suddenly, inexplicably there. "It's me." His words came as a whisper, clear as anything in my left ear. I would know his voice anywhere.

"It's me." His words came as a whisper, clear as anything in my left ear. I would know his voice anywhere.

I thought I was hearing things. I thought I was making things up. I thought if it really was him he had come some four years after his death just to tell me I had spent too much money on fabric. That would be just like him, even dead, to make a snarky comment.

Surely ghosts have better things to do... don't they? And how could he be a ghost here, in a house where he had never been in life? Don't ghosts need to have "imprinted" themselves on a place in order to haunt it or, at the very least, follow psychic breadcrumbs? I didn't know how he got here or if I liked that he had.

Why here? Why now? Why me? Over the next several weeks, dim thing that I am, I began to notice that Larry "visited" only in the dining room, which soon after I moved into the house had been converted into my sewing room. Every time I stretched out fabric, considered patterns, or otherwise settled in to work in the sewing room I was soon joined by Larry. We were practically companionable. At first, it was just his presence that I felt, as if I were to turn around I would see him standing there, alive as anything.

What I saw was not a ghostly image of my dead ex-husband. That would be too easy. I did see images... the flutter of a shadow passing from one room to another, the outline of a hand withdrawing from the corner of my eye. Once, at one end of my sewing counter, I saw a familiar plaid shirt peeking out from beneath a folded length of wool. But when I approached to inspect it more closely, it was gone. The images were fleeting, the voice barely more than a whisper. Did I really see him? Hear him? Maybe I was just losing my mind. What ex-husband wouldn't want to facilitate the insanity of an ex-wife? And to do so from the grave, so much the better. Except I was so comforted by his presence. Adrian would soon be coming home from college and I bore a motherly worry over his future. Had I stopped at all the right parental touchstones? Had I reminded Adrian the requisite number of times to wear clean underwear, to be polite to old people, to write thank-you notes even for gifts he considered obtuse? Surely I had done everything I knew to do and Mr. Dead Dad over there had gotten off the hook as it were, his being dead and all.

That was it. Larry wasn't really here, I was just jealous of his being dead and of my having to pick up the slack, take the heat if Adrian turns out to be a screw up. Jealous of a dead guy… pitiful.

I found myself returning again and again to the dining room, just in case. He wasn't always there. Though it was usually little more than a feeling, more and more often there were hints, secrets. Like the button jar – the buttons kept in a small jelly jar had been emptied onto the sewing counter. All that remained in the jar were a few pfenig, German coins. Early in our married lives we had lived in Germany. For years afterward we would find a few pfenig in coat pockets, change purses, in the camera pouch and diaper bag. There isn't much you can do with foreign coins, so I thoughtlessly tossed them into the button jar, which now sat empty on the counter except for those few pfenig – less than five marks in change. If I had any doubts about whether the voice and the fleeting images being the ghost of my dead ex-husband, those German coins assured me that Larry really was here, in my house.

I have never been sure what it is Larry has been trying to say. Is he just lonely? Bored? Is he trying to tell me something significant about Adrian? At first, I feared that he was here to warn me that something terrible would happen to Adrian if I didn't unravel his meaning and intercede. But I didn't figure out anything and nothing terrible did happen. Adrian has returned from college, gotten a job, moved into his own apartment, gotten engaged and just recently married…so far so good. I will say that the week I spent making my dress for Adrian's wedding was a companionable one with Larry. I heard his whisperings twice and found two more pfenig. Whether they are the same old bits of change or are new pieces I haven't bothered to discern. The dress turned out well. Maybe he's here to help me sew.

What does Larry mean coming here? Is he here to tell me something or is there something for me to tell him? Maybe he just wants to know that Adrian's doing good. You would think that once you divorce somebody and they are dead...well, I guess that isn't the end of it, is it?

In addition to the ghost of her ex-husband, Jenny Durbin enjoys the company of two cats, two dogs and a very lively boyfriend who is practically perfect in every way.

About Angela Hoy

Angela Hoy is the author of nine non-fiction titles. She and her husband, Richard, are the owners of WritersWeekly.com (a site that publishes free paying markets and job listings for writers) and Booklocker.com (a publisher of print and electronic books).

Angela and Richard live on the Penobscot River in Bangor, Maine with their four children, Zach, Ali, Frank and Max.

Do You Have a Story to Share?

If you would like to share your experiences, read the experiences of others, participate in discussions, or learn more about spirit communication, please visit Angela's website today at http://www.SpiritStories.com.

If you wish to contact a licensed medium, please contact the National Spiritualist Association of Churches at http://www.nsac.org/churches or the Worldwide Directory of Spiritualist Churches at http://www.lighthousespiritualcentre.ca/Churchdirectory.html.

CPSIA information can be obtained
at www.ICGtesting.com
Printed in the USA
FSOW02n0038260617
35616FS